SWINDON
WORKS
THE LEGEND

SWINDON
WORKS
THE LEGEND

ROSA MATHESON

Cover illustrations. Front, top: GWR Works entrance, Swindon; bottom: At work in Swindon Works. *Back*: *clockwise from top left*: The women of the Trimming shop, Carriage & Wagon Works; The iconic 'hooter'; *King George V*, now a preserved heritage piece at the National Rail Museum, York. (Bob Townsend Photographs)

First published 2016

The History Press
The Mill, Brimscombe Port
Stroud, Gloucestershire, GL5 2QG
www.thehistorypress.co.uk

British Library Cataloguing in Publication Data.
A catalogue record for this book is available from the British Library.

ISBN 978 0 7509 6624 5

Typesetting and origination by The History Press
Printed and bound in Great Britain by TJ International Ltd

CONTENTS

ACKNOWLEDGEMENTS

I always love this part of the book, acknowledging the kind and generous help given by friends old and new. It pleases me that my books are a collaboration of shared passion.

So once again warm appreciation goes to Elaine Arthurs, archivist at STEAM – Museum of the Great Western Railway; to Daryl Moody, Lead, Local Studies at Town Centre Library; and Sophie Cummings, Curator at Swindon Museum and Art Gallery. All couldn't have been more helpful. Thanks to Wiltshire and Swindon History Centre and to those at St John's Ambulance HQ.

BIG thanks to good friends and fellow authors who always give encouragement and assistance – Rev. Canon Brian Arman, Ken Gibbs and Andy Binks. Special thanks to John Walters and Bob Townsend, whose knowledge, resources and generosity have helped many books be achieved, mine included; not forgetting the Thursday morning gang in STEAM Museum and those at the Thursday Railwaymen/women's Club; as always, couldn't have done it without you. Thanks also to the 'enthusiasts' who let me quote from their websites – John Ward, Andrew Grantham and Brian Basterfield. Special thanks to my mate-in-crime, Jack Hayward, always there for me no matter what, and to the 'Friends' on Swindon Works Training School Facebook page for their enthusiasm and responsiveness. An acknowledgement of the work of Alfred Williams must also be added.

SWINDON WORKS

Appreciation to my commissioning editor, Amy Rigg, for her boldness and willingness to help make this happen and my publishers for their sense of adventure in trying something new. As writers and publishers of history we have, I believe, a duty to bring this history to new and younger audiences, as well as faithful followers, so that the history of their forebears will not be lost so we try something 'new'.

The last thanks, as always, go to my wonderful family for their continued support and interest in my railway work, particularly grandson Evan, whose passion for railways – 'diesels, signals and points *and* signal boxes' – gives us both a great deal of pleasure.

SWINDON WORKS: THE BEGINNING ...

The starting point was the fact that the Great Western Railway Company was in need of a factory to repair its bought-in locomotive rolling stock. The Board of Directors gave the task of finding the location for such an establishment to their young engineer Isambard Kingdom Brunel and he gave the job to Daniel Gooch, his assistant but who was to become the first Locomotive Superintendent at Swindon Works. In the words of Daniel Gooch:

> **1840.** During this year further portions of the Great Western were opened and agreements were made for leasing the Bristol and Exeter and the Swindon and Cheltenham Railways, and it became necessary to furnish large works for the repair, etc., of our stock. I was called upon to report on the best situation to build these works, and on full consideration I reported in favour of Swindon, it being the junction with the Cheltenham branch and also a convenient division of the Great Western line for the engine working. Mr. Brunel and I went to look at the ground, then only green fields, and he agreed with me as to its being the best place.

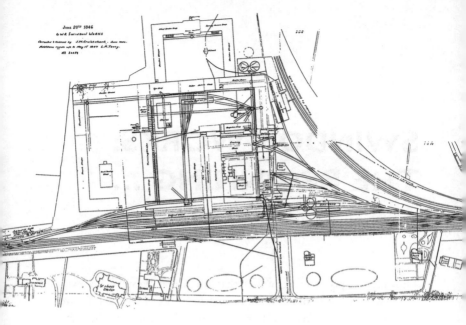

1841 plan.

Gooch then wrote to Brunel in September 1840 that, having put his mind to the task of the best site for the 'principal engine establishment' and having 'studied the convenience of the Great Western Railway, only':

> an engine establishment at Swindon commensurate with the wants of the Company, where a change of engines may be advantageously made ... The establishment there would also comprehend the large repairing shops for the Locomotive Department.

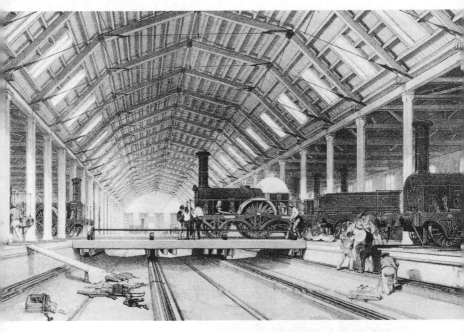

J.C. Bourne's iconic lithograph of the engine house at Swindon in 1846. A 'Firefly' class locomotive stands on the traverser receiving attention from 'the mechanicals' or 'mechanicians'.

His recommendation was endorsed by the directors, who on 25 February 1841 authorised the construction of such a depot at Swindon in the following words:

> Decide to provide an engine establishment at Swindon commensurate with the wants of the Company, where a change of engines may be advantageously made and the trains stopped for the purpose of passengers taking refreshment. The establishment there would also comprehend the large repairing shops for the Locomotive Department.

and sometime shortly after, work began.

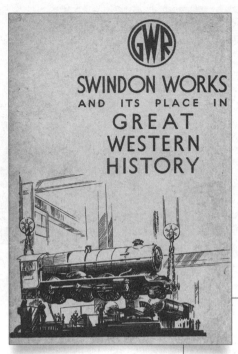

SWINDON WORKS
AND ITS PLACE IN
GREAT
WESTERN
HISTORY

SWINDON WORKS
AND ITS PLACE IN
BRITISH
RAILWAY HISTORY

PUBLISHED BY THE RAILWAY EXECUTIVE
(WESTERN REGION)
PADDINGTON STATION, LONDON, W.2

1950

1

WHAT WAS SWINDON WORKS?

Swindon Works was ...

IN THE WORDS OF ...

In the words of Works employee, **Alfred Williams**, as stated in the title of his iconic book (1915), it was simply:

> *The Railway Factory.*

In the words of **Sir Daniel Gooch**, then Locomotive Superintendent, in 1847:

> Swindon [Works] has been designed and built to employ 1,800–2,000 men, and all the arrangements of tools and shops have been made to employ that number of men to the best advantage ...

For most the Works is always thought of in three sections – Locomotive. Carriage. Wagon. Locomotive came first. Carriage and Wagon came together later, and so are always said in one breath but, in the words of *Astill's Almanac and Trade Guide: New Swindon 1872* – it is something other:

> The G.W.R. Railway Works are situated on the north side of the Main Line. The three Establishments constituting what is

known as 'the Works', viz: *The Locomotive Works*, *The Carriage Manufacturing Department*, and *The Rail Mills* are carried on under one general management and are unique in their arrangements.

In the words of the Company's General Manager **Frank Potter** in 1910:

> Swindon [Works] throughout the Great Western Railway and in many other quarters beside, is a synonym for all the qualities and characteristics which were associated with the broad-gauge – thoroughness, solidity and substantiality – and the expression of that idea is to be found today, in this, the seventy-fifth year of the GWR, wherever the locomotives, the vehicles, or appliances of any kind, manufactured at Swindon, are in use. It does not matter how small or comparatively trifling the article maybe, if it has been made at Swindon, it needs no legend to be stamped upon it to indicate the place of its origin or manufacture.

In the words of **Mrs Violet Joynes**, who worked 'Inside' during the Second World War, it was:

> A town within a town – it had its own buses and bus stops even!

In the words of two who worked there in its dying decades of the 1970s and '80s:

> **Nigel George**: The centre of a much loved empire.

> **Mark Buckley**: An engineering and manufacturing power-house; a school of knowledge; a family. A way of life!

Whilst in the words of **Ian Williams** (the great-great nephew of the aforesaid Alfred Williams):

> The Works was one huge storybook where almost everyone knew everyone someway or other.

MANY THINGS ...

Swindon Works was originally a depot for stabling engines which were changed at Swindon before the train continued on to Bristol; its workshops were for their maintenance and repair work.

Swindon Works was Great Western Railway Company (1841), British Railways Western Region (1948), British Railway Workshops (1962), British Railway Engineering Ltd (1970).

Swindon Works was Broad Gauge, Standard Gauge, Steam and Diesel.

Swindon Works was sheds, shops, foundries, mills, stores, laundry, offices, sidings, 'houses', 'works', yards, turntables, bus routes, tunnels, bridges.

Swindon Works was people: artisans, mechanics, contractors, machinemen, apprentices, tradesmen, engineers, female sewers, firemen, shunters, labourers, boiler-makers, helpers, strikers, under-chargemen, chargemen, under-foremen, foremen, managers, checkies, clockies, shop clerks, office clerks, female clerks, draughtsmen, messenger boys and girls, Chief Clerks, Works' Managers, Locomotive, Carriage & Wagon Superintendents, CMEs, CM&EE.

Swindon Works was apprenticeships and training – acknowledged worldwide.

Swindon Works was a way to work – '*there was everyone else's way and there was Swindon's way.*'

IN THE WORDS OF WRITERS AND COMMENTATORS

1847

We cannot pretend to go through the works in details for ours was but a flying visit. The works are of a vast extent, and when the meal time is announced, and the men turn out to attend the sober duties of the victualing office, you are astonished at their number. An entire regiment of comfortable, well-clad and intelligent men, bear evidence of 'a fair day's wage for a fair day's work'. They are one thousand in number. The works is divided into different departments. The machinery is of the most ingenious and powerful description.

Devizes and Wiltshire Gazette, 25 February

1852

Swindon, all-important Swindon; who that knows aught of railways, or railway travelling, has not heard of Swindon's world-wide reputation … for the vastness of its workshops and engine-depot.

George Measom, publisher and philanthropist,
Illustrated Guide to the Great Western Railway

1861

It seems the works are beginning to assume the importance which those qualified to judge had for years stated must be the result of the plant, already established, in the immense pile of buildings, which had, however, for years had little activity in them. The time, however, has, it appears, arrived, and the workshops are rapidly filling with men. Further, there have been within the past few months great additions to the works in the shape of 'rolling mills' (we believe they are called) for railway metals.

'The Great Western Railway Works at Swindon',
Devizes and Wiltshire Gazette, 2 May

1890

Certainly the largest centre of railway industry in England, and probably in the world. [A proud boast that would be repeated down several decades!]

The Great Western Railway Magazine, November

1933

I had never been to Swindon before and all I knew about it was that the Great Western Railway had its chief works there and that it made the best railway engines in the world.

Writer J.B. Priestley, on visiting the town

1950

The whole works covers 326 acres, a formidable figure for intending visitors. To see the locomotive shops thoroughly involves a walk of some 7½ miles. ... were the Works transferred to the north Thames embankment in London they would stretch from Waterloo Bridge to Vauxhall Bridge. At the same time the gas works would trespass across St James Park to Pall Mall, the foundry would be on the site of Westminster Abbey and the carriage stock shed would lie across the Tate Gallery.

British Machine Tool Engineering, April–June

1983

Swindon Works was one of the largest single assets of the GWR and its fortunes and misfortunes through the years were closely connected with the short-term and overall policy of the Board of directors of the Company at any period.

Alan Peck, *The Great Western at Swindon Works*

MEN OF CALIBRE

Men who put Swindon Works 'on the map':

Locomotive Superintendent

Daniel Gooch	1837–1864

Locomotive, Carriage & Wagon Superintendent

Joseph Armstrong	1864–1877
William Dean	1877–1902
George Jackson Churchward	1902–1916

Chief Mechanical Engineer

George Jackson Churchward	1916–1921
Charles Benjamin Collett	1922–1941
Frederick William Hawksworth	1941–1949

Mechanical & Electrical Engineer		Carriage & Wagon Engineer	
K.J. Cook	1950–1951	H. Randle	1950–1951
R.A. Smeddle	1951–1956	C.A. Roberts	1951–1956

Chief Mechanical & Electrical Engineer

Robert Alfred Smeddle	1956–1962

Locomotive Works' Managers		Carriage & Wagon Works' Managers	
G.J. Churchward	1896–1901	T.G. Clayton	1868–1873
F.C. Wright	1901–1902	J. Holden	1873–1885
H.C. King	1902–1913	C.J. Churchward	1885–1895
C.B. Collett	1913–1920	L.R. Thomas	1895–1901
W.A. Stanier	1920–1922	T.O. Hogarth	1901–1902
R.G. Hannington	1922–1937	F. Marillier	1902–1920
K.J. Cook	1937–1947		

Locomotive Works' Managers (cont)		Carriage & Wagon Works' Managers (cont)	
H. Randle	1947–1948	C.C. Champeney	1929–1922
C.T. Roberts	1948–1952	H.G. Hannington	1922–
J. Finlayson	1952–1956	E.T.J. Evans	1922–1946
A.S. Smith	1956–1960	H. Randle	1946–1947
S. Ridgway	1960–1962	C.T. Roberts	1947–1948
		H.G. Johnson	1948–1962

Chief Works' Manager

J.S. Scott	1962–1967

Locomotive Works' Manager		Carriage & Wagon Works' Manager	
H.W. Mear	1962–1967	E.T. Butcher	1962–1963

Works' Managers

H.W. Mear	1967–1972
H.R. Roberts	1972–1981
H. Taylor	1981–1986

WHO IS MISSING?

One notable GWR name is missing from the above listings: Isambard Kingdom Brunel. The reason for this is that Brunel played no role in the internal management of the Works and visited it but a few times, and rarely once he stopped designing engines. The significant role he did play in the Works was as an architect.

ICONIC STEAM ENGINES

Great Western 2-2-2
Iconic broad gauge engine

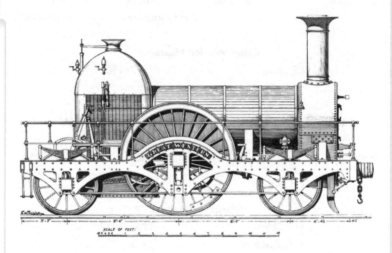

SCALE OF FEET:

❖ Designed by [Sir] Daniel Gooch to the GWR's Board demand 'to build a colossal locomotive working at full speed' – by working day and night it took only thirteen weeks from drawing board to final testing.

❖ First complete build by GWR at Swindon Works. Outshopped April 1846.

❖ 1 June 1846 ran Paddington to Exeter – 194 miles in 208 minutes – returned in 211 minutes.

❖ Wheel arrangement 2-2-2 – outside slotted sandwich frames – wheelbase 8'0" + 8'0".

❖ Massive driving wheels 8ft in diameter.

❖ Later wheel arrangement altered to 4-2-2.

❖ Its basic design became basis of the GWR's Broad Gauge express locomotive stock.

- Worked for twenty-four years.
- Scrapped (unbelievably) December 1870 – after running more than 370,000 miles.

The Lord of the Isles 4-2-2

Daniel Gooch's most famous and celebrated engine

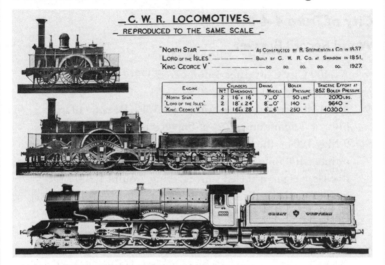

- Broad Gauge 'Iron Duke' Class – for Express Passenger work.
- Twenty-two engines in this class were built at Swindon Works. *Lord of the Isles,* built March 1851, was the last …
- and the fastest and most powerful Broad Gauge locomotive. 'It was the Concorde of its day', to quote Brian Arman, Broad Gauge author and expert.
- Certainly Gooch's most exhibited engine – at the Great Exhibition, Hyde Park 1851, Edinburgh 1890, Chicago, USA, 1893, and finally Earl's Court 1897.
- With its symmetry of design and excellent performance it has been called 'one of the handsomest engines ever constructed'.
- Famous 8ft driving wheels.
- Two pairs of leading wheels and one pair of trailing wheels 4ft 6in in diameter.

- 18in x 24in cylinders,
- Working steam pressure of 115lb.
- Tenders with water capacity of 1,760 gallons.
- Ran 789,300 miles with original boiler intact.
- Started work July 1852. Withdrawn from service 1884.
- Broken up 1906 after several rejections for preservation.

City of Truro 4-4-0

World Record Breaker

- A 3400 City Class (later renumbered 3700) designed by G.J. Churchward and built in 1903.
- No. 3440 later became renumbered 3717. Because of its historical significance *City of Truro* has been preserved.
- 9 May 1904 – the first locomotive to reach and pass the magic number 100 miles per hour! From Plymouth to Bristol, pulling five large eight-wheeled vans carrying around 1,300 large bags of 'ocean mail' making an estimated load of 148 tons *not* including engine and tender, between Whiteball Tunnel to Wellington.
- Just west of Taunton, reached its top speed of 102.3mph! (164.6 km/h) as registered by independent timekeeper Charles Rous-Marten, who wrote for the *Railway Magazine* (this speed was and is challenged).

King George V 4-6-0

A GWR Giant

- Designed and produced by C.B. Collett CBE, Chief Mechanical Engineer.
- The 'first' in this exciting new 'King' Class Express Passenger Locomotive, No. 6000, named after the reigning King. Others would be named after previous kings in backward chronological order.
- Named by some as 'weighty-puffers' as, because of their tonnage, they had to be restricted from some lines.

The "King" of Railway Locomotives

G.W.R. EXPRESS PASSENGER LOCOMOTIVE "KING GEORGE V"

" King George V " is the first of the Great Western Railway Company's " King " class of locomotives, the most powerful passenger train engines in Great Britain.
Designed and produced by Mr. C. B. Collett, C.B.E., Chief Mechanical Engineer of the Great Western Railway, in the Company's Locomotive Works at Swindon.

Cylinders (four)—Diameter .. .. 16¼ in.	*Boiler Pressure* .. .. .. 250 lb. per sq. in.	*Wheels*—Bogie, diameter .. .. 3 ft.	
Piston Stroke .. 28 in.	Barrel length .. .. 16 ft.	Coupled .. .. .. 6 ft. 6 in.	
Heating Surface total .. .. .. 2,514 sq. ft.	Barrel diameter (outside) 6 ft. and 5 ft. 6¼ in.	*Water Capacity of Tender* .. .. 4,000 gallons	
Grate Area .. .. 34.3 sq. ft.	Firebox length (outside) 11 ft. 6 in.	*Weight of Engine and Tender* (in working order) 135 tons 14 cwt.	
	Tractive Effort at 85 per cent. B.P. 40,300 lb.		

(David Hyde Collection)

✧ Made to a deadline to be GWR's standard bearer at the Baltimore and Ohio Railroad Centenary, it required three-shift working around the clock on some components but was completed within the six months. Then she had to be partially dismantled again for the boat trip! Chargeman Fred Williams and Fitter George Dando, who had built her, went over to do the re-assemble.

✧ Maiden trip on the Cornish Riviera Express in July 1927.

✧ 'The greatest and most powerful locomotive ever constructed in this country.' – *The North Devon Journal*, 7 July 1927.

The Great Bear 4-6-2

A Stand Alone Engine

✧ 1908 'Pacific' No. 111 – the first of this type to be used on British rails and remained the only one for fourteen years. The 'one-and-only' produced by GWR.

✧ Designed by G.J. Churchward, whose aim was 'to develop a boiler that would be much in advance of the GWR's traffic department later needs' (according to O.S. Nock), the enormous boiler had a length of 23ft and a diameter of 5ft 6in.

✧ The locomotive with a weight of 97+ tons had a nominal tractive effort of 27,800lb.

✧ A 'Special Red' coding restricted it to the Paddington to Bristol run because of its heavy axle loading.

✧ Desired for prestige by the Board of Directors, loved by railway enthusiasts, disliked by Collet, it had a mighty presence and glamour appeal.

✧ Withdrawn in 1924 and parts used to build a 4-6-0 in the Castle Class, and given the name *Viscount Churchill* although it retained its number – No. 111. It was withdrawn in July 1953.

The much loved and historic *Evening Star*.

DID YOU KNOW?

'A' SHOP

1900

New 'A' shop – GWR Board allocated a massive £33,000 – housing Erecting, Fitting and Repairs as well as Boiler and Machine shops.

The Engineer on the 1904 visit of the Institution of Mechanical Engineers:

> New Erecting Shop (480 feet by 306 feet). This is the latest and most up-to-date building in the works. It is equipped throughout with electric power. There are two electric traversers and four rows of engine pits holding 80 locomotives. The western row of 20 pits is used for new work, and the others for repairing passenger engines. There are four overhead hydraulic electric cranes, each having two 25-ton lifts and two 21-ton quick lifts. The heavy lifts are by hydraulic power, worked by 8-H.P. electric pumps. There are independent motors for traversing movements, 33 H.P. and 2.5 H.P. Compressed air is available at any point in the shop, and is in general use. The shop is lighted by 700 c.p. are-lamps, and by glow-lamps at the benches and pits. Gas is also laid on. Capacity-80 to 90 DOW engines and 500 repaired engines per annum.

1935

Grace's Guide – British Industrial History: 'Swindon Works and its Place in Great Western Railway History':

> The principal shop is the 'A' Erecting and Machine Shop, the area of which is 502,975 square feet, and undoubtedly *this is one of the finest locomotive shops in the world*. The main idea underlying its planning was to provide for progressive operations connected with locomotive erecting, fitting, and wheeling.
>
> It really comprises four sections, known respectively as 'A' Erecting Shop, 'A' Machine and Fitting Shop, 'A' Boiler Shop, and 'A' Wheel Shop. [A(E), A(M), A(V), A(W)]

PLANS 1900–56

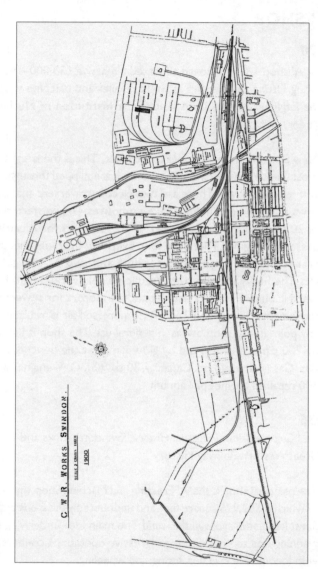

G W R WORKS SWINDON.
SCALE 2 CHAINS 1 INCH
1900

1900 plan.

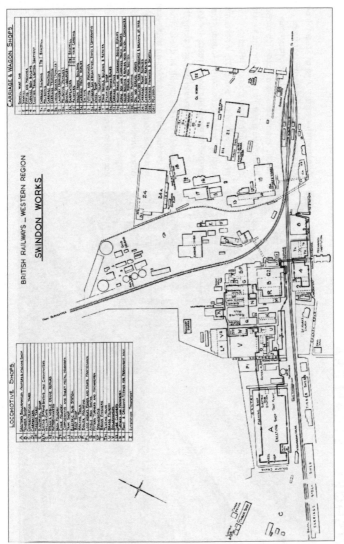

BRITISH RAILWAYS – WESTERN REGION

SWINDON WORKS

1956 plan.

27

WORKSHOPS – STEAM ERA

Nineteenth-century 'Age of Steam' Iron Foundry where dirt floors, hot fires, molten metals, toxic fumes, nauseous smells, even explosions, made it a most hazardous place. No wonder the Works' cats wouldn't stay there! This early photograph of the south bay, where small castings were made, shows foundrymen preparing moulding boxes ready for the pour. Molten iron was brought along the walkway from the cupola at the far end of the foundry in crucibles on trolleys to make the pour. On the left is the shop office where the clerical staff, workshop inspectors and the foremen were accommodated.

WORKSHOPS – DIESEL ERA

Twentieth-century Iron Foundry (north bay) in the 'Age of Diesel', becomes 9 Shop – a transformation – now so clean compared to its previous existence. Even the 'smells' would have changed! Here we can see power units and transmission from various locomotives. Items at front right – two automatic gear boxes, two reconditioned AEC 1,500hp diesel horizontal engines and second trailer is of crankshafts of either cleaned or machined DMUs. (David Hyde Collection)

Swindon Works was ...

STEAM AND DIESEL

In the mighty A Shop c. 1930s in the Age of Steam Locomotives – Class 6100 2-6-2T side tank engines Nos 6159 and 6157 under construction. The batch 6150–6159 had a small but significant alteration to the original design in the use of 225psi boiler pressure, which increased the tractive effort from 24,300lb to 27,340lb.

The AE (Erecting) Shop, during the 1960s. Dieselisation was to change the railway scene forever, which eventually brought dramatic physical changes to the workshops, particularly in respect of cleanliness. Immediate front is a D7000 series 'Hymech'. Made in the Works with a Maybach V16-cylinder engine (1,750bhp), it was used mainly for pulling freight. Behind this is the 'Western' series, which had two Maybach engines each developing 1,350bhp. D1031 *Western Rifleman* lines up in front of D1000 *Western Advocate*. All main line services would be pulled by these new locos.

BRITISH RAIL ENGINEERING LTD.
Integrated Loco & Carriage Workshops
Proposed Re-organisation 1981
not implemented. 93 Acres.

1981 plan.

SHOP	ACTIVITY
1	TRAIN HEATING
2	TRANSMISSION
3	MACHINING
4	COPPERSMITH & SHEET METAL
5	ELECTRICAL TRACTION
6	DIESEL LOCO REPAIRS
7	LOCO BOGIE WHEEL & FINAL DRIVE
8	DIESEL TEST STATION
9	DIESEL ENGINE REPAIRS
10	BRASS FOUNDRY
11	BRAKING EQUIPMENT
12	WAGON & CONTAINER REPAIRS
13	STEEL FABRICATION
14	B.R.I.T.E.
15	SMITHS & BUTT WELDERS
16	HEAT TREATMENT
17	WIRE ROPE & CHAIN TEST
18	SPRINGS
19	DIESEL MULTIPLE UNIT REPAIRS & BATTERIES
	BOSH & PAD HOUSE

SHOP	ACTIVITY
20	CARRIAGE & WAGON BOGIE WHEEL & FINAL DRIVE
21	CAR REPAIRS
22	CRANE REPAIRS (WAS O.D.M. & C.C.E.V EQUIPMENT)
23	GRIT BLAST & PRIME PAINTING (WAS LOCO RECEPTION)
24	WHITE METAL FOUNDRY
32	TOOL ROOM
33	MECHANICAL MAINTENANCE
33	MAINTENANCE GARAGE
33	'X' BOILER STATION
34	DIESEL TEST STATION
35	BUILDING MAINTENANCE
36	ELECTRICAL MAINTENANCE
37	FIRE STATION
38	SCRAP RECOVERY & INCINERATION
39	PATTERNS & PLASTICS
53	YARD & GENERAL LABOURERS
54	WORKS TRANSPORT GARAGE
	NO. 1 SUBSTATION

STORES	DESCRIPTION
70	BOLTS, NUTS, SPRINGS
71	STEEL PLATE, BAR, TUBE & BINDING CHAINS
72	B.R.I.T.E.
73G	GENERAL DOMESTIC ITEMS; SCREWS, PINS.
74	NON-FERROUS CASTINGS
75	POISONS
73G	TOOLS, GRINDING WHEELS
76	D.M.U. TRIMMING, PULLMAN, FINISHERS.
77C	WAGON MATERIALS
77R	WAGON MATERIALS
77V	MODIFICATION KITS
78	MASONS
78	PAINTS
79	TIMBER
80	ERECTION & FITTING, MECHANICAL
82	GEAR BOXES
83	TRANSMISSIONS
84	FINAL DRIVE, ELECTRICAL, OIL.
85	DIESEL ENGINES
86	BRAKE GEAR
87	CRANE

STORES	DESCRIPTION
88	FERROUS & NON-FERROUS SCRAP
88	TRAIN HEATING
90R	DIESEL LOCO, REPAIRABLE
91R	BRAKE GEAR, REPAIRABLE
92R	ENGINE, REPAIRABLE
92R	STORES OFFICE
93R	ELECTRICAL, REPAIRABLE
94R	PATTERN
...	LICENSED (PART OF 76 STORES)
	OFFICES, ETC.

GENERAL OFFICES & TELEPHONE EXCHANGE
MANAGER'S OFFICES
DIESEL TRAINING SCHOOL
AREA LABORATORY
CANTEEN & MEDICAL CENTRE
LONDON STREET MAIN ENTRANCE
WESTGATE ENTRANCE RODBOURNE RD
APPRENTICE TRAINING SCHOOL

RAILWAYMEN

Railwaymen in the 'Age of Steam'

These men – Boulton, C. Whateley, H. Blake, W. Bullock, J. Cook, J. Lintern, J. Knox, I. Brown, H. Hinder (these names were hand-written in this order on the back of the photograph, presumably by Hooper), staring boldly at the new phenomena of a camera, being photographed by William Hooper, a fellow railwayman, circa early 1900s in Brunel's B Shed – worked at the cutting edge of technology delivering GWR's ground-breaking steam engines. (Paul Williams' Hooper Collection)

Railwaymen in the 'Age of Diesel'

Diesel engines required a new set of skills. The new Diesel Engine Shop was, ironically, started up in the old B Shed, and became BD Shop – the shop of the 'new-era'. Roger Hayes, left, measuring a connecting rod bearing and John Smith, right, examining the piston, which have just been removed from the very first Maybach 1,100bhp 12-cylinder engine re-conditioned in the Works 1961.

DID YOU KNOW?

TESTING PLANT – THE FIRST IN EUROPE

In 1904 the first Locomotive Testing Plant in Europe was built in the Works, designed by G.J. Churchward, then Locomotive Carriage & Wagon Superintendent. The *Great Western Railway Magazine* wrote.

> It consists of a 'bed' made of cast iron, bolted on a concrete foundation with timber baulks interspersed for the lessening of the vibrations. ... intended not only for the purpose of scientific experiment but also to do away with trial trips of new and repaired engines.

It had five pairs of carrying wheels that were adjusted to suit different locomotives by racks and pinions driven by an electric motor. The axles of these wheels had band-brakes, water-cooled, and worked by small hydraulic cylinders, which were supplied by a motor driven return-flow pump.

It was rebuilt in 1936 and special additions and moderations over the decades facilitated extensive advancements and developments.

2
FASCINATING FACTS AND FIGURES

Numbers: The Workforce

1843

The Works employed **423** men, of which **72** were highly skilled engineers. (Daniel Gooch, diary)

The PRO holds a document that identifies the first railwaymen engaged at the Works in 1843:

Foremen	6
Clerks (Time Office and Stores)	14
Enginemen	48
Firemen	50
Stationary Enginemen	3
Cleaners, Coke men, Labourers, etc.	65
Fitters & Erectors	55
Turners	10
Contractors	60
Men at Machines	7
Carpenters and plumbers	6
Coppersmiths	2
Brass Foundrymen	1
Blacksmiths	14
Springmakers	2
Strikers	14

Boilermakers & Wheelmakers	4
Painters	2
General Labourers	25
Boys	35

1847

By 1847 the number of workmen had increased to **1,800**.

1848

The Great Western Railway Company have **discharged 250 men** from their Works and the whole of the men employed at their factory are now working on short-time, and probably the men will have to remain on short-time the whole of the winter.

Devizes and Wiltshire Gazette, Thursday 21 September

1852

The Works of the Great Western Railway Company have increased the number of their hands at the Factory in the Town and are working full time. There are about **eleven hundred workmen** now employed there.

Reading Mercury, Saturday 29 May

1857

We regret to find that the discharge of workmen is still going on from the company's works at New Swindon, a large number of men having already been discharged on Saturday last, to meet this great reduction, we hear all new work has been suspended for the present. ... The number of mechanics etc., already discharged exceed **400**. We understand that a further reduction is to take place on Saturday next.

Reading Mercury, Saturday 12 September

1869

We understand from Mr. Ellis, the manager, there are about **three hundred and ten** hands employed in these works. These hands are divided into two 'shifts' the one to work by day, the other by night, the night work being taken alternate weeks by all the men …

> 'Notes of a Night Visit to the New Swindon Puddling
> Furnaces and Rail Mills'
> *The Swindon Advertiser*, Monday 1 March

1872

… the total number of artisans, etc., employed is about **3,900**, and the fortnightly paylist at the present time exceeds the large sum of £9,000 *exclusive* of the salaries of the staff of superior officers of the various establishments.

> *Astill's Almanac and Trade Guide: New Swindon*

1892

LOCOMOTIVE DEPT:	
Locomotive factory	5,000
Rolling Mills	300
Running Sheds	300
	<u>5,600</u>
Saw Mill	400
	<u>2,200</u>
WAGON WORKS:	1,000
OFFICE STAFF:	300
STORES DEPT: PLATELAYERS &	350
	<u>10,050</u>

> *The Town and Works of Swindon with a Brief History of*
> *the Broad Gauge*

1905

A return of 24 June gives a total employment of **8,365** in the locomotive works, and **5,081** in the carriage and wagon department, while **750** more were working in the traffic, stores, and permanent-way department – more than **14,000** staff altogether. (Ex. Inf. Mechanical and Electrical Engineer's Office)

1910

14 July 1910

NUMBER OF MEN REGISTERED AND WAGES PAID

The total number of men registered in the Locomotive & Carriage Department

on	25 June 1910	was 26,475
and on	26 June 1909	was 27,694

a decrease of 1,219 made up as follows:

Swindon Works	592
Outstation	627
Total	1,219

SWINDON WORKS

Total number of men registered in Swindon Works:

28 May 1910	**10,971**
9 July 1910	**10,976**

an increase of 5, as under:

Locomotive Works, increase	15
Carriage & Wagon Works, decrease	10
	5

Signed   G.J. Churchward.

1912

Report – Swindon Works, 7 March 1912

Total number of men registered, Swindon Works:

2 March 1912	**12,316**	28 December 1912	**12,297**
4 March 1911	11,271	30 December 1911	12,150

an increase of 1,045 made up as follows:

an increase of 147 made up as follows:

Locomotive Works	406	Loco Works	decrease	52
Carriage & Wagon Works	639	C & W	increase	199
	1,045		increase	147

Signed   G. Churchward

In 1912 the coal miners mounted the first National Miner's strike demanding a minimum wage. It started in February and ended on 6 April, lasting thirty-seven days, placing many other industries that depended on coal in a critical situation – especially railway workers:

WORK FOR LOCOMOTIVE MEN

Having been informed on Friday last that they would be 'locked out' until sent for the **7,000** odd employees in the **locomotive department** of GWR Swindon works have been summoned to work by a notice which stated that the department would be open from 9 o'clock this Wednesday morning until 5.30 Friday evening so that practically the same amount of employment is being found for the men this week as has been the case for the past fortnight.

Gloucester Citizen, Wednesday 20 March 1912

1924

In 1924 the Works employed **14,369** people. It was the most it had ever employed. After this began a slow, creeping contraction.

1926

The petition to supply electricity to the Works sets out that these Works employ **13,000** persons …

Western Daily Press, Thursday 11 March

1931

826 MEN DISMISSED

GWR is giving notice to 1,300 men. Eight hundred and twenty-six from Swindon where 125 will leave the Chief Mechanical Engineer's Department 325 the Locomotive works, and 376 the C & Works …

Men aged 65 and over will be retired. This affects 181 of which 125 are at Swindon …

'All companies are having to cut down their staff owing to falling off in business ... We employ about **12,000** men at Swindon alone so the dismissals are not large compared to the numbers employed.'

Gloucester Citizen, Saturday 25 July

1934

1,300 MEN TO LEAVE THE WORKS
BELT SYSTEM TO BE INTRODUCED

Four hundred men **(400)** employed in the locomotive department of the Great West Railway works at Swindon received notices terminating their service in a week's time. It is learned on good authority that **900** others will be discharged at intervals during the next six months.

The 'belt-system' is to be introduced at Swindon as at Crewe. Under this system it is understood it takes only 12 days for a locomotive to pass through the shops compared to 30 days under the old system.

The Citizen, Saturday 11 August

1938

Reasons for dismissal of **1,140** men employed in the Carriage, Wagon and Locomotive departments at GWR's Swindon works are stated to be falling receipts and the increased costs of materials.

Western Times, Friday 27 May

Friday 27 May 1938 was remembered by the workers as 'Black Friday'.

1948

At the time of Nationalisation there were around **4,300** men employed in the Carriage & Wagon Dept., and **6,100** men on the Loco side.

1962

The Evening Advertiser **February 1962** reported that there were twenty-eight shops in the Works and **4,550** employees, only a few hundred more than there had been in 1875.

1965

Swindon Works' Annual Report for 1965 recorded that there were **2,140** skilled men, **1,582** semi-skilled and **481** unskilled employed there – a total of **4,203.**

1969

Railway repair workshops like those at Swindon face the bleakest future. **170** men in loco repair may lose jobs in July from total workforce of **3,886.**

The Evening Advertiser, January

1981

British Rail Engineering Ltd
Proposed Re-Organisation of Swindon Works

Phase B
November 1981

Wages Staff – Categories of Labour and Numbers Employed

	Cat 4	Cat 3	Conciliation	Cat 2	Cat 1	Apps	Total
Production Shops							
Total	1,397	145		284	127	128	2,081
B&Q Service Shops							
Total	236	93		187	90	39	645
Other Staff							
Total	2	1	31	2	2	118	155
Grand total Staff	1,635	238	31	473	219	285	2,881

1986

26 March: 'Black Wednesday'

1,100 workers left in disconsolate dribs and drabs. **450** were left to 'mop-up' over the next twelve months. The 'official' closure date for Swindon Works was 31 March 1986 (Easter Monday). There would be no more Swindon Works' railwaymen.

DID YOU KNOW?

The Rule Book

GREAT WESTERN RAILWAY.

RULES AND REGULATIONS

TO BE OBSERVED BY

WORKMEN EMPLOYED IN THE WORKSHOPS

OF THE

LOCOMOTIVE, CARRIAGE AND WAGON DEPARTMENTS.

1. Every applicant for employment must be in good health, and will only be temporarily engaged until a satisfactory character has been received from his last employer for whom he has worked six months. He must produce his Certificate of Birth, and must sign a declaration that he has read a copy of these Rules, and that he undertakes to observe and be bound by them as a condition of his employment. *Condition of Service.*

2. The usual hours of work are as follow :— *Hours of work.*

Monday to Friday	6.0 a.m. to 8.15 a.m.
	9.0 " " 1. 0 p.m.
	2.0 p.m. " 5.30 p.m.
Saturdays	6.0 a.m. to 8.15 a.m.
	9.0 " " 12. 0 noon

totalling 54 hours per week, or an average of nine hours per day.

The infamous GWR Rule Book ruled the life of their 'Company servants'. It laid out the terms and regulations of the railwayman's working life. Each workman was given their own little book specific to *'the Workshops of the Locomotive, Carriage & Wagon Departments'* which, upon entry to the Company, they had to sign to say they had *'carefully read (or had them read to me)* and *clearly understood them'* and to signify their agreement to *'bind myself to observe and obey the foregoing Rules and Regulations'.*

The rules, set up primarily for administration reasons, were also to control the workforce, as well as minimise accidents, avoid physical disasters, prevent misuse, wastage or theft of materials and assist production, although not necessarily in that order.

The number and severity of the rules differed at different times. The Rules of 1874 lists only twenty-four, whilst those of 1904–1916 lists thirty-nine separate items. Many of these Rules attracted 'punishments', usually fines or suspension and loss of pay, the ultimate punishment being 'dismiss without notice' – in GWR times that would also mean loss of your home if you lived in the Company houses! The GWR Rule Book persisted up until its demise in 1947.

After Nationalisation there were a number of significant differences in the new Rule Book. Now it was called *Resolution of the Railway Executive* (1950) and later the *Resolution of British Railways Board* (1972) and addressed to 'employees' rather than 'servants'. The sub-parts of each rule became far more numerous and, while fines disappear, 'suspension' is applied to more situations as in matters of misconduct, negligence, or disobedience to superiors. Other disciplinary practices such as loss of job are continued. Some rules such as not bringing intoxicating liquor to work, absence from duty without permission and returning (or not taking) company property, span the time.

The general consensus of those who worked 'Inside' is that post 1960, while the rules existed, and there were a lot of them, there was a lot more leeway given. One could receive a number of 'verbal warnings' before any 'actions' were taken, and now, of course, one had the unions on one's side!

Names and Trades

In early days the 'names' given to the different workers simply reflected the nature of the work they did, especially in the 'hot-shops':

- ✧ roughers
- ✧ knocker-out
- ✧ drag–out man
- ✧ die sinker
- ✧ roller and ladle runner
- ✧ stay–tapper
- ✧ pull–up boy
- ✧ washer-downer
- ✧ cushion–beaters

Though some make one wonder:

- ✧ chaff–cutter
- ✧ dings separator
- ✧ shingle

An early(ish) GWR Wages Statement for the Carriage Department gives us some idea:

GWR Carriage Department 8 July 1871

Sawyers	17
Timbermeasurers	5
Machinemen	25
Turners	2
Fitters	11
Strapmakers	2
Enginemen	3
Saw Sharpeners	1
Steam cranemen	1
Coachmakers	132
Underframe makers	10
Lifters	24

Wood Wagon Builders	52
Gas Fitters	1
Trimmers	32
Sewingmachinemen	2
Carpenters	12
Painters	47
Polishers	8
Tinmen	2
Fishers	45
Bricklayers	2
Smiths & Strikers	31
Masons	2
Iron wagon builders	17
Platelayers	4
Examiners	3
Greasers	3
Labourers	235

The 1943 ABC of Railwaymen

This list of the different grades who had volunteered for the Works' Home Guard shows a grand total of 154 roles:

A   Analysts, Angle Iron Smiths, Apprentices, Armature Winder, Axlebox Trimmer, Axle Turner

B   Batteryman, Blacksmith, Blacksmith's Asst., Boiler Attendant, Boiler Attendant Asst., Boilerscruffer, Boilersmith, Boilersmith's Asst., Boilerwasher, Brakebox Fitter, Bolt Maker, Bolt Repairer, Brake and Drawgearman, Brass Finisher, Brickarchman, Bricklayer, Bricklayer's Buffer

C   Callman, Case Hardener, Carpenter, Carriage Repairer, Carriage Cleaner, Carriage Fitters, Carriage Fitter's Asst., Carriage Lifter, Checker, Piecework etc., Clerk, Coach Bodymaker, Coach Finisher, Coach Trimmer, Coalman, Coppersmith, Coppersmith's Asst., Crane-man and Crane-Driver, Coremanker

D   Draughtsman, Driver

E   Electrical Fitter, Electrician, Electrician A.T.C., Engine Cleaner, Erector, Examiner, Elec., Examiner Carr & Wagon

F   Firedroppers and Fire Cleaners, Firelighter, Firewatcher, Fireman, Fitter, Fitter's Asst., Floorlayer, Forgeman, Forgeman's Asst. Furnaceman, Furnaceman's Asst.

G   Gas Fitter, Gas Fitter's Asst., Gas Maker, Gland Packer, Grease Maker & Oil Blender, Greaser, Gaugeman

H   Hammer Boy, Holder-up, Hydraulic Engineman, Hydraulic Repairer, Hydraulics Labourer, Hydraulic Fireman

I   Inspector – Boiler, Inspector – Material, Inspector – Shop

L   Labourer, Lamp Attendant, Lead Burner, Lifter, Lifter's Asst.

M   Machinery Attendant, Machinist, Machinist Boy, Main Layer, Messenger, Millwright, Moulder

P   Packing Splicer, Painter, Patternmaker, Photographer, Pipe Fitter, Pipe Layer, Plater, Plater's Asst., Platelayer, Plumber, Polisher, Porter – Office, Pumpman, Puncher & Shearsman

R   Rigger, Rivet Hotter, Rivetter

S   Saddler, Scaffolder, Saw Doctor, Sawyer, Sawyer's Asst., Shunter, Sheet Metal Worker, Shift-Engineer, Shedman, Spotter (Roof), Stationary Engineman, Steam Hammerman, Steam Raiser, Storesman, Striker, Stripper & Cleaner, Sub-Station Attendant, Switchboard Attendant

T Timber Marker, Timekeeper, Tinsmith, Toolman, Tube Cleaner, Tuber, Turner

V Vacuum Brake Examiner

W Wagon Builder, Wagon Repairer, Wagon Repairer's Asst., Wagon Rivetter, Wagon Writer, Watchman, Water Pumping Engineman, Water Fitter, Weighman, Welder, Wheel Turner, Wheelwright, Window Attendant, Wireman, Wood Machinist, Wood Machinist Boy, Wire Ropeman

DID YOU KNOW?

They Made Their Own

Oil and grease (and those who made them) rarely figure in the story of locomotives and railways, but such lubricants (and workers) were essential for the smooth running not only of the machinery of the Works but also of its products – carriages, wagons and locomotives – without them everything would grind to a halt. Different types were needed for different jobs. It made economic sense for the GWR and BR to make their own as they used tons of it – in 1954 the Works were producing 6,000 tons of lubricating oil and 460 tons of axle grease for use throughout the Western Region. The 'management' of these products was extensive. In the 1950s the movement of oil stocks, the reception and despatch of oils, greases, empty drums etc., involved the use of some 4,250 wagons a year.

A small internal by-product produced in the Oil and Grease Works was the 'sand-soap' issued to the workmen for scrubbing clean their hands and forearms. Made of sand (yes) and oil (very little of this according to the men) it was issued in a small tin, which could be brought back and topped up as was needed. This abrasive cleaner, used over many decades and by successive generations, may have accounted for some of the skin problems encountered in the Works generally.

The Oil and Grease Works was closed in 1964.

Apprenticeships

What was an apprenticeship? Although the time spent as an apprentice changed over the decades from seven to five, to three and finally two years, the ethos that shaped apprenticeships remained much the same.

There was definitely more to 'apprenticeship' than learning a set of skills and technical know-how. It was the 'preparation time' that took a 'schoolboy' and turned him into a 'skilled working man'. His path took him from 'boy' to 'apprentice' to 'tradesman'. Along the way he 'learned' other, and, some say, as important things, about the workplace, its culture, its hierarchy and *his* changing place in it. He learned the codes of conduct that said what was acceptable and what was not in terms of his thinking, appearance and behaviour, both in the workplace and outside; this was especially true of Swindon Works as 'outside' was truly an extension of 'Inside'.

Whilst apprenticeship was an entry to the workplace it was also a barrier. It guarded access to skills-specific labour markets. The 1563 Statute of Artificers under Queen Elizabeth I, which sought to fix prices, impose maximum wages and regulate training, made apprenticeship compulsory and prerequisite, decreeing that no one who had not served an appropriate apprenticeship for a specified number of years was allowed to become a 'Tradesman'. 'Skill' defined a tradesman. 'Minors' were 'bound over' by means of a legal Indenture to a 'master' guaranteed by a parent or guardian. The terms and condition of early indentures would be considered extremely onerous today as they restricted personal as well as professional liberty. 'Indentures' became a very emotive word, full of fear – and pride.

From its beginnings, and as it grew and changed, the Works provided opportunities for boys in many trades – some that lasted its lifetime, but also some new and unheard of at its birth.

Just as the Works changed, so did apprenticeship, until, as some said, it became unrecognisable; it became something completely different. One thing that never seemed to change, however, were the apprentices – their nature, attitudes, irreverence, seemed to pass from one generation to another. They were another 'legend' of the Works.

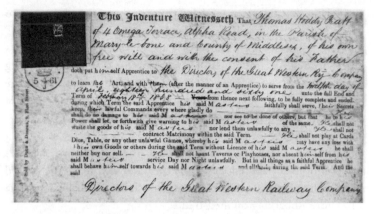

This is a most unusual Indenture in that it is the only one that I have come across where the apprentice is apprenticed to *the Directors of the Great Western Railway Company* rather than to just an individual such as the Superintendent or the Manager or to 'the Company'. Thomas Hoddy Pratt must have had very good connections.

Apprentices in Swindon Loco Workshops 'Given Up' 1878–1893

Year	Jan	Feb	Mar	Apr	May	Jun	Jul	Aug	Sep	Oct	Nov	Dec	Total
1878	6	6	3	1	1	3	3	6	3	4	2	3	41
1879	5	5	1	3	1	3	3	4	5	3	11	5	49
1880	6	6	4	3	7	2	1	3	3	3	8	7	53
1881	7	4	7	7	2	7	4	1	4	5	6	3	57
1882	8	7	7	2	10	7	4	2	8	14	10	8	87
1883	4	9	12	7	14	8	13	8	19	12	7	7	120
1884	10	11	13	6	5	4	6	7	11	12	8	5	98
1885	10	9	9	10	9	8	13	9	4	6	6	4	97
1886	3	11	11	6	7	9	8	8	9	8	4	3	87
1887	8	12	5	10	9	16	8	8	9	9	9	12	115
1888	7	9	11	13	12	18	16	16	10	15	13	14	154
1889	17	17	12	8	13	23	16	19	16	14	11	17	183
1890	16	18	15	15	14	14	7	12	16	7	11	13	158
1891	13	1	19	12	11	10	8	12	10	10	15	11	130
1892	7	13	14	12	11	7	3	3	2	0	1	3	76
1893	13	12	7	8	12	11	14	14	6	8	9	5	119

'Given Up' was the term used for those apprentices who were no longer bonded, i.e. they had completed their apprenticeships.

There were two 'official' ways into apprenticeship in GWR's time – through a family member working for GWR or by paying a 'premium', i.e. a fee. Views of those who have gone through the system are divided into two camps; one holding that 'it was the best possible way of learning a trade' while the other describes it as 'slave' or 'cheap labour'.

Both works – Loco and C & W – had 'their own ways', routines and traditions for apprentices. Boys on Loco side would be started mainly in the Scraggery turning nuts, a much hated, boring, repetitive job, before embarking on their trade.

Cavan Moroney, Loco side:

I was a Fitter/Turner/Erector Apprentice which was a Loco Works trade. First port of call for Loco side turners was 'The Scrag' in the R shop where we received sack upon sack of blank nuts and bolts produced in the Stamp Shop. We spent our lives putting the threads on these. They were all big Whitworth sizes. Draw hooks were produced by the blacksmiths in the Stamp Shop and turned in the R Shop by apprentices. The Brass Foundry survived well into the '70s producing white metalled bearings for freight wagons.

John Attwell, 1940s C & W:

Although it was not hard and fast we were moved in a fairly organised way. Apprentices always started on No 1 gang, which was a light job based in a siding outside the shop where we had to refurbish drop light windows. This meant removing the drop lights and the mouldings, which would be repaired inside, and then re-glazing the windows prior to fitting them back in the coach. After three months we were moved to a gang that undertook more complex work. The work got a little more complex with each move.

The 'practice' of apprenticeship was for the boy to gain all kinds of work experience to acquire the necessary knowledge and skills and so he was moved around the workplace at 'regular' intervals, although this could depend on need of the Company and the skill of the boy. This was the same in the time of the GWR and British Rail.

Jack Harber, fitter-turner-erector, apprenticeship started 1932:
During my apprentice the erecting shop work practice was altered from a strip-and-rebuild on the same pit and by the same erectors, to a sectionalised flow system of four sections. Apprentices spent two months on each section working on one side of the locomotive fitting the repaired parts, by this time the apprentice was now a skilled workman and capable of working with a minimum of supervision. The final section was the finishing off and trial section. Trials were generally to Dauntsey and back. The last shift was to the new construction. During the time I worked on there, it was more conversion than new work: Class 5200 2-8-0 T to Class 7200 2-8-2 T and Class 4300 2-6-0 to Class 6800 4-6-0.

Few things disrupted apprenticeship – ill health, absconding (a lot of this in the nineteenth century), lay-offs (at hard times even apprentices were not immune) and wars. Wars complicated apprenticeship and agreements between governments, unions and tradesmen had to be reached.

A New Era
Upon Nationalisation in 1948 in British Railways' time 'premiums' were no longer required.

Big Changes
The type of apprenticeships available changed over the years as old skills gave way to new technology, tin smiths, for example, grew into sheet metal workers. In the mid-1960s big changes were made to apprenticeship and its delivery – the ATS, Apprentice Training School.

Work is due to begin on Monday on an £180,000 school for railway works' apprentices in Swindon. The school is the first of its training type to be built in the Western region. It is hoped

BRITISH TRANSPORT COMMISSION

BRITISH RAILWAYS

APPRENTICESHIP AGREEMENT

This Agreement made the................................day of
....19.... BETWEEN ....
....

on behalf of the **BRITISH TRANSPORT COMMISSION** (hereinafter called "the Commission") of 222, Marylebone Road, St. Marylebone in the County of London of the first part, and..
.... of

in the County of..(hereinafter called "the Guardian")
of the second part, and..
....of ....
....in the County of................................
(hereinafter called "the Apprentice") of the third part.

   WHEREAS—

  1. The Apprentice has completed a period of probation from the
....day of..19.... to the
....day of..19.... and has attained the age of 15 years.

  2. The Commission are willing to accept the Apprentice to be taught and instructed in the craft of..

  3. The Guardian having enquired into the nature of the business conducted by the Commission desires that the Apprentice shall learn the craft of..in the service of the Commission.

   Now it is hereby AGREED as follows:—

  (1) The Apprentice, of his own free will and with the consent of the Guardian, hereby binds himself as Apprentice to the Commission in the craft of..on the conditions hereinafter appearing.

On many levels this document represents not only the end of an era and long traditions, but also the beginning of a brave new world, with bright, new hopes and aspirations.

the building will be ready by spring 1962. It will incorporate a single storey workshop covering 11,000 sq feet fully equipped to prepare the boys for the type of work they will do when they pass on to the works. Other facilities in a 2 storey block include a lecture room, a library, a common room, and staff accommodation and a combined assembly hall, gymnasium and cinema.

The Evening Advertiser, September 1960

The major step-change introduced by this new approach was that the first year was 'off-the-job' and 'in-the-school' and the philosophy and methodology had changed from 'learning through practice' to 'learning by instruction.' 'Production' was no longer an intrinsic part of the training but 'nurture' was. The aim was to produce not just a good craftsman, but also a good citizen. Another big change was that the boys had a 'try-it-and-see' period to assess their strengths, skills and interests *before* deciding on their trade. This was also known as a 'probation period'.

Gordon Dickinson:

Life in the training school was fun, hard work, but really interesting. For the first few months we all spent a period of time on each of the different trade sections, i.e. Sheet metal,

The 'shop floor' in the training school was nothing like that in the factory workshops – here, bright, clean and orderly; there, smells, noise, dirt and grime of many decades. Here there were four sections: nearest front is machining; next is fitting; further back electrical fitting; and sheet-metal working. Behind the back door (left) was welding and behind the right, moulding.

carpentry, electrical engineering, machining, etc. Each section being run by an experienced tradesman, who would have spent several years in 'The Works'.

These 'choices' were also based on the needs of the Works, whether they needed so-many fitters, or electricians or other trades, which they would communicate to the principal/chief instructor of the ATS.

Works Annual Report 1965
1.5 Apprentices Training
The number of apprentices and trainees as at 31 December 1965:

	Loco	C&W	Total
Blacksmithing	-	3	3
Boilermaking	2	5	7
Carpentry & Joinery	4	3	7
Coch Bodymaking (with Finishing experience)	-	8	8
Coach Finishing (with Bodymaking experience)	-	7	7
Coach Painting	-	3	3
Coach Trimming	-	2	2
Coppersmithing	9	3	12
Electrical Fitting	24	1	25
Engineering	4	1	5
Fitter, Turning & Erecting	179	5	184
Gas Fitting & Plumbing	2	3	5
General Fitting & Turning	-	31	31
Moulding	2	-	2
Painting (C.E.M)	2	3	5
Painting (Engine)	2	-	2
Painting (Maintenance)	1	-	1
Patternmaking	2	-	2
Sheet Metal Working	1	-	1
Wagon Rivetting	-	3	3
Wood Wagon Building	-	7	7
Total	**234**	**88**	**322**

TRAINEES

	Loco	C&W	Total
Holding-up	–	1	1
Metal Machining	9	10	19
Wheel Machining	–	1	1
Wood Machining	–	4	4
Welding	3	–	3
Total	**12**	**16**	**28**

Training

From early times 'training' was a separate classification to 'apprentice-ship', although all apprentices were 'trained'. What defined each was the level of skill required. What (and who) defined the 'level' of the skill was always an area of tension. It was widely acknowledged in the Works that 'machining' was a highly skilled job but it had a Grade 2 classification and did not warrant an apprenticeship. Paradoxically the 'Tool Room' was the prestigious shop and those who worked there – machinists – were highly regarded by all for their level of skill.

What is interesting in this list of 'trades' is the reduced number of 'trades' on offer – 1943 = 154 whilst 1965 = 21.

'Night school' (generally much hated by the boys after a hard day's graft) was now no longer a compulsory element of the apprenticeship, as the 'schooling' was done in-house with the teachers coming to ATS.

In all periods meticulous log books of work undertaken were kept and marked, as well as a record of total training:

Geoffrey Fletcher
Record of Practical Experience 1963–68 [this was a little red book]

Works Training Scl	basic craft practice
Machine Shops	general turning including automatic, turret, centre lathes, etc.
Fitting Shops	general locomotive detail fitting including diesel engine repair shop
Erecting Shop	diesel locomotive erecting and repair

Diesel Training Scl	diesel traction (mechanical) course
Diesel Testing St.	engine and transmission testing
Welding School	basic welding practice

Over the years ATS morphed into the WTS – Works Training School ('apprenticeship' slips from the vocabulary). From 1970 'Certificates' carry the BREL heading. As with the Works, the WTS comes under

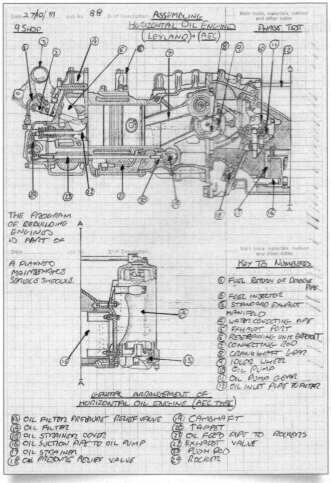

Malcolm Holland's log book drawing: 9 Shop Phase test, 27 October 1981. (Malcolm Holland)

threat of closure. In an attempt to keep going the WTS then offered 'Youth Training Schemes' but limited in range – just three:

1. General Maintenance.
2. Electronic and Mechanical Assembly.
3. Warehouse and Storekeeping.

Whether 'apprenticeship' or 'training', GWR or British Railways, what everyone needed at the end was 'the Certificate' – a revered piece of paper. It proved you had 'done it'. In all eras it carried a 'character reference', almost word for word it remained the same:

> 'Surname' bears a good character, possesses good ability as a workman and has conducted himself in a satisfactory manner.'

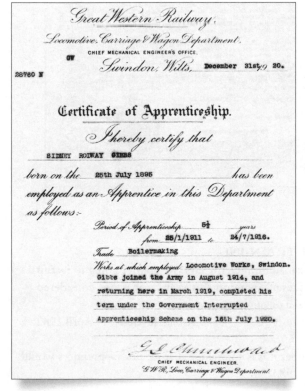

It is interesting to compare the style of wording and presentation of these two certificates, one for apprenticeship and one for training, under the different ownerships and managements. Note that Sidney Gibbs' includes time interrupted by war service.

Bad News

NO MORE TRAIN-ING

BREL spokesman from Derby says 'We are not going to recruit any apprentices at Swindon this year … it is not considered prudent to take on any youngster.'

The Evening Advertiser, 19 April 1982

Later in November it was confirmed that no new apprentices would be taken on for 1983/84.

The Last Apprentice
Ryan Conduit, 1986:

On the Last Day I had been called up to the training
department to finish my Apprentice Log Book and hand it
in. I can remember being there all day finally finishing it, then
handing it into Gerry Pontin, who took it to Ken Dann for
final signing off. As he came through the door the final long
hooter that was ever to sound started to blow.

'Well,' he told me, 'You're the last in a very long line. The last
apprentice this Works will ever produce.'

The training given at Swindon Works became 'legendary' in its
own lifetime. It is often quoted that 'an apprenticeship (or training)
completed in Swindon Works was a passport to employment
anywhere in the country' – or the world.

DID YOU KNOW?

HOURS WORKED

Each Certificate of Apprenticeship or Training carried the number
of hours involved as in this one of **Lewis Gustav John Lockyer
Sondermann**.

Year	Ended	Hours Works Open	Hours Worked	Special Leave	Illness	Without Leave	Total
July	1928	2299	2285½	13	--	½	13½
	1929	2290½	2201¾	7¾	81	½	88¾
	1930	2371½	2303*	39	47	½	86½
	1931	2214	2127¾	86¼	--	--	86¼
	1932	2147	2103	44	--	--	44
Totals	5 years	11322	11021*	190	128	1	319

* includes 18 hours' overtime.

DID YOU KNOW?

HIERARCHY

The Great Western Railway Company had a complex structure of hierarchy that was imbued into every part of the organisation. It was evidenced in level of command, level of work, level of skill, level of service. It was so imbued that in the Works everything – shops, gangs and offices – all had a hierarchy. Hierarchy determined status. Hierarchy determined pay. This situation did not change when it came under British Railways, although the 'authority' became a little more relaxed.

Skill
Unskilled – semi-skilled – skilled: This was the most contentious, highly sought and highly prized hierarchy on the shop floor.

Shop Floor
Boy – apprentice – journeyman – leading-hand in gang – under-charge man – chargeman – inspector – senior inspector – temporary foreman – foreman – head foreman – superintendent.

Stores
Heavy gang (basic labourer) – Warehouse Staff – Warehouseman – Foreman – Office Personnel – Deputy Purchaser – Senior Purchaser

Trades
Top-of-the-trades Loco-side was fitter-turner-erector, C & W side it was carriage body-maker.

Gangs
'New-Work gang' was a good gang to be on as was the 'Finishing gang' but top-gang was the Maintenance Gang. This was a go-anywhere, do-any-job gang, and usually only for long-time servers.

Visitors

The Works was an instant 'attraction' right from its beginnings, drawing people from every background and walks of life not only from all over the British Isles but the world, too. The range of visitors down the years would make a book in itself – company directors, enthusiasts, royalty (our own and foreign), politicians, celebrities, learned associations, rock bands and TV programmes to cite just a few. The GWR itself organised Works' excursions, while in later years many loco-spotter clubs and tour operators organised their own visits, too. Wednesdays were the traditional 'Open Day' but access could be obtained on other days upon application to the Staff Office. It really was extraordinary that visitors were allowed at all in this most dangerous workplace, but they were and 'visits' continued right to the end:

> The extensive works of the Great Western Railway at this place, were inspected by a large body of the directors Friday last, and in the evening they attended with Mr Saunders, Mr Brunel and a large party of friends connected with the company, a Music Performance in the School House.
>
> *Devizes and Wiltshire Gazette*, Thursday 15 April 1847

In June 1847 the British Association for the Advancement of Science and Technology held their seventeenth Session at Oxford and as part of their conference the gentlemen members paid a visit to Swindon Works. They were greatly taken not only by the cutting-edge technology but also by the 'calibre of the men'.

21 May 1856

NOTICE TO VISITORS

It is particularly requested that no gratuity is offer by visitors to the attendant. If the attendant receives a gratuity instant dismissal will be the consequence upon it being reported.

<u>Signed</u> – Minard Rea, Manager.

N.B. There is a Mechanics Institution in connexion with the Establishment. Donations are thankfully received.

THE WHEEL AND STEAM HAMMER SHOPS

The Steam Hammer has always been an object of attraction for visitors to the New Swindon Factory. There are ten Steam Hammers. But there is one amongst the lot that is spoken of as *the* Steam Hammer. It is a King amongst the hammers and the workmen are justly proud of it. Its head weighs four tons ... at one blow it will annihilate a mass of iron and send it flying in million of sparks far and near, or it will play with it and tap it as a coquettish lady would strike your cheek with her fan, or pat it as a cat would pat a mouse and then by way of change, devour it.

The Swindon Advertiser, 1 May 1871

Institution of Mechanical Engineers: Visits to Works: 1877

On Friday, 27th July, an Excursion was made by a free special train to visit the Great Western Railway Locomotive and Carriage Works at Swindon, through which the Members were conducted by the Chairman of the Railway Co., Sir Daniel Gooch, and the locomotive superintendent, Mr. William Dean; and they were handsomely entertained at luncheon in the Works.

The special train conveying the Members to Swindon was fitted with Sanders' Automatic Vacuum Brake, applied to most of the vehicles in the train, and its action was illustrated by some quick stoppages at high speed that were made in the course of the trip.

Grace's Guide to British Industrial History

On the invitation of the President *Mr Spagnoletti**, the Society of Telegraph Engineers and Electricians on Tuesday visited the GWR Swindon Works. A special train of carriages conveyed some 400 men from Paddington to Swindon in time for lunch. Arrived at the destination they found luncheon laid out in the large volunteer drill hall in connection with the Works … a few toasts were proposed and drank and brief speeches in reply …

[the visitors were told] 'our Works is not an exhibition, so proceed carefully.'

Western Daily Press, 2 July 1885

* Charles E. Spagnoletti, M.Inst.C.E., M.Inst.E.E. He joined the GWR as its first Telegraph Clerk in 1855 and eventually became its Chief Electrician & Telegraph Superintendent, and remained in this post until his retirement due to ill health.

VISITORS TO SWINDON WORKS

Commencing Monday 28th Sept, Visitors to the Works who are not employees, will be charged 3*d* for each person. The employee on obtaining the usual Metal Pass will receive the required number of tickets for his friends.

No person will be allowed to visit the Works unless accompanied by an accredited guide. These regulations apply equally to *night visitors* to the Rolling Mills.

September 1903

This charge remained the same until after the Second World War, when it went up to 6*d*. By the 1960s it was free.

Distinguished Visitors

King George V and Queen Mary

Tuesday 28 April 1924 marked the first Royal visit to the Works. Their tour took one hour:

3.15 p.m.: Enter works by Sheppard Street entrance

Inspect:
Laundry
Polishing and Finishing Shops
Carriage Bodymaking
Saw Mill
Iron Foundry
Engine Being Turned on balanced Turntable by One Man
Types of Engine in Yard
Engine Testing Plant
Lifting Complete Engine by Overhead Crane
Wheel Shop
Wheel Balancing
Weighbridge and Engine being Weighed

4.25 p.m.: entrain Royal Saloon (outside Weighbridge House)

In the Iron Foundry they watched work in progress on a huge floor casting – it was a special 'Welcome' commemorative plaque of their visit.

The King, accompanied by the Queen on the footplate, 'drove' the appropriately named *Windsor Castle* locomotive attached to the Royal Saloons from the Works back to the station.

Writing later to Viscount Churchill, their Majesties said they were 'gratified' to have had the 'opportunity of becoming acquainted with this vast industrial centre'.

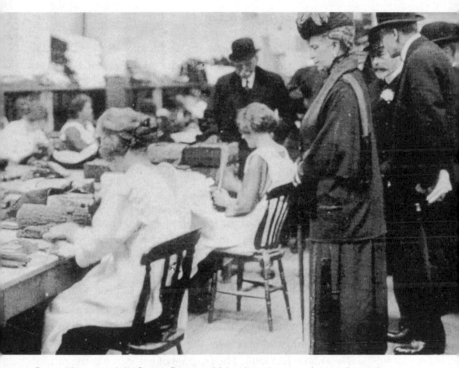

Queen Mary visited the Sewing Room and (*above*) can be seen admiring the work
of the girls who produced netting for the carriage luggage racks. Immediately behind
her is the CME C.B. Collett, and then King George V.

King Amanullah of Afghanistan

King Amanullah visited the works on Wednesday 21 March 1928. To mark the occasion, the GWR produced a Persian language commemorative booklet, containing an illustrated history of Swindon works and portraits of the Company's Chairman, Deputy Chairman, General Manager and Chief Mechanical Engineer, C.B. Collett.

Collett accompanied King Amanullah on his visit who 'with his customary keenness and untiring energy, manifested the liveliest interest in everything he saw' and kept the CME busy answering questions through an interpreter.

The King inspected the footplate of newly built Locomotive 6009 *King Charles II*. At the close of the tour, a 'large number of workpeople [gave] the distinguished visitor three hearty cheers, which seemed to please him.' (*The Railway Gazette*, 23 March 1928, p.387)

HRH Princess Elizabeth

The future queen visited Swindon on 15 November 1950 as part of the Borough of Swindon's (established 1900) Jubilee Celebrations. She travelled from Paddington on the 'Star'-class Locomotive No. 4057 – *The Princess Elizabeth*. The purpose of her visit was the official naming of Locomotive No. 7037 *Swindon* as part of Swindon's Jubilee celebrations. She also received a model of it.

The *Swindon*, built under the umbrella of British Railways, was the last in the line of GWR's famous 'Castle'-class express passenger engines to be built at the Works. Designed and delivered by C.B. Collett, the Chief Mechanical Engineer, when first introduced the 'Castle' class was heralded as Britain's most powerful express passenger locomotive. (Later, F.W. Hawksworth, the new CME, modified the boiler, which made the engine even more effective.) The *Swindon* was given the unique honour of being the only engine to have splashers decorated with Swindon Borough's own Coat of Arms.

K.J. Cook (Mechanical & Electrical Engineer 1950–51) recalled that the following Saturday the Works was opened to all and some 20,000 people took the same tour HRH had.

BRITISH RAILWAYS   WESTERN REGION

SWINDON
RAILWAY NEWS

END PRODUCT

VOL. 1. No. 1. APRIL, 1960

At a time when theatres, cinemas and soccer clubs are playing to diminishing audiences, the drawing power of Swindon Works increases. 26,080 visitors arrived last year. Many come by rail and this means valuable revenue estimated at £7,500 annually. Wednesday is Open day. No permits are required and, subject to age restrictions, anyone can come. There are two queues: one party of fifty or sixty for the extended tour. Number taking is discouraged with this group as it causes delay on a tight schedule. 'Spotters' for the short tour begin to form up on the other side of the entrance as early as 1.30 p.m.. It is not an orderly gathering being largely composed of boys. There are big boys, small boys, neat boys, scruffy boys, fat boys, thin boys, dirty boys and (a few) clean boys. *Swindon Railway News*, 1960

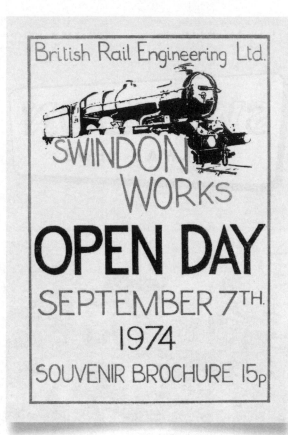

British Rail Engineering Ltd.

SWINDON WORKS

OPEN DAY

SEPTEMBER 7TH.
1974

SOUVENIR BROCHURE 15p

A Visitor's View

6 November 1976

My first recorded visit to Swindon appears to have been on a cloudy 6 November 1976 when the Works contained many Class 52 Westerns and some Class 24s. Like most trips to the Works it started out by going through a gateway, under the mainlines and then up alongside one of the main shop buildings before entering the main erecting shop area. Swindon's workload at this time focused on diesel multiple units, refurbishing of Southern Region electric multiple units,

Class 03 and 08 overhauls and repairs to hauled stock. After passing through the erecting shops it would be out into the yards, where much stock and locomotives could be found, usually awaiting scrapping. Then it was back through the areas that looked after the diesel multiple unit repairs/refurbishings.

10 August 1980

The summer of 1980 opened up a new chapter in the events at Swindon Works and this visit on August 10th 1980 gave a clue as to what the future held. The Works was still busy with Class 08 and diesel multiple unit repairs. Unclassified repairs were still taking place to visiting Classes, at this time 25218, 45023 & 45053 were received for repairs. However, elsewhere in the Works were three withdrawn Class 25s and at least one Class 46 that would herald the reawakening of Swindon as a location for the storage and disposal of retired locomotives.

(from www.derbysulzers.com/in.html)

LOCOMOTIVES: AN ENTHUSIAST'S RECORD

B.R. Basterfield on Visits to Swindon Works and Shed, 1953 & 1964

On this visit to Swindon Works, there was excellent representation of Great Western steam motive power to be seen. The two Gas Turbine locos, 18000 and 18100, seemed to spend more time in works than out. In fact I never saw either working a train. The Works tour had to be rushed, following our late arrival. The Works loco listings are likely to be incomplete. It is also probable that locomotives seen passing on the main line have been included in the works listings. As a 14 year old, my only ambition was to note the numbers and underline them in my ABC. We had a group photograph taken on 70022 Tornado. If only I still had it.

Visitors

B.R. Baterfield's Locomotive Records, 1953
SWINDON SHED & STOCK SHED (82C)

70016 Ariel

4097 Kenilworth Castle
5009 Shrewsbury Castle
5010 Restormel Castle
5022 Wigmore Castle
5062 Earl of Shaftesbury
5070 Sir Daniel Gooch
5084 Reading Abbey
5091 Cleeve Abbey
7015 Carn Brea Castle
7025 Sudeley Castle
7037 Swindon

1004 County of Somerset
1011 County of Chester

4062 Malmesbury Abbey

6832 Brockton Grange

4907 Broughton Hall
4912 Berrington Hall
4916 Crumlin Hall
4925 Eynsham Hall
4951 Pendeford Hall
4967 Shirenewton Hall
4972 Saint BridesHall
4992 Crosby Hall
5922 Caxton Hall
5934 Kneller Hall
5949 Trematon Hall
5959 Mawley Hall
5967 Bickmarsh Hall
6935 Brownsholme Hall
6965 Thirlestaine Hall
6973 Bricklehampton Hall
6975 Capesthorne Hall
7914 Lleweni Hall
7923 Speke Hall

90152 (2-8-0)	78008 (2-6-0)	5226 (2-8-0T)	3682 (0-6-0T)	9790 (0-6-0T)	1428 (0-4-2T)
90312	78009		3684	9795	1446
		4538 (2-6-2T)	3725		
2818 (2-8-0)	46525 (2-6-0)	5509	3780	7424 (0-6-0T)	5802 (0-4-2T)
2852	46527	5510	4612		5804
2855		5534	5755	2060 (0-6-0T)	5805
2865	2224 (0-6-0)	5540	5770		5806
3825	3213	5564	6739	1366 (0-6-0T)	5807
		5566	8793	1367	5812
4375 (2-6-0)	2474 (0-6-0)	5574	9600	1369	5814
5327			9629		5817
5396	9008 (4-4-0)	8436 (0-6-0T)	9720	1336 (2-4-0)	
6320	9010	8472	9721		W27 (Railcar)
6384	9020	9400	9773	5 Portishead	
6391	9026	9476		(0-6-0)	
TOTAL 107					

SWINDON LOCOMOTIVE WORKS & YARDS

6001 King Edward VII
6010 King Charles I
6011 King James I
6020 King Henry IV
6021 King Richard II
6022 King Edward III
6027 King Richard I
6028 King George VI

70022 Tornado

1013 County of Dorset

4080 Powderham Castle
4084 Aberystwyth Castle
5001 Llandovery Castle
5013 Abergavenny Castle
5015 Kingswear Castle
5035 Coity Castle
5076 Gladiator
5078 Beaufort

5090 Neath Abbey
5099 Compton Castle
7005 Lamphey Castle
7006 Lydford Castle

4003 Lode Star

4908 Broome Hall
4926 Farleigh Hall
4968 Shotton Hall
4971 Stanway Hall
5906 Lawton Hall
5981 Frensham Hall
5999 Wollaton Hall
6936 Breccles Hall
6966 Witchingham Hall
6996 Blackwell Hall

6806 Blackwell Grange

7823 Hook Norton Manor

75030 (4-6-0)	3022 (2-8-0)	3153 (2-6-2T)	4510 (2-6-2T)	8737 (0-6-0T)	2148 (0-6-0T)
75031	3034		4512	8779	2167 (0-6-0T)
		4151 (2-6-2T)	4527	9626	2195
90585 (2-8-0)	6305 (2-6-0)	5138	4581		
90676	6318	5196	5511	5402 (0-6-0T)	1436 (0-4-2T)
	6379				1442
2802 (2-8-0)	7320	6123 (2-6-2T)	8479 (0-6-0T)	1709 (0-6-0T)	
2823		6146		1991	207 (0-6-2T)
2867	2354 (0-6-0)		3674 (0-6-0T)	2038	309
3843	2409	4273 (2-8-0T)	4631	2067	344
		4288	4679	2122	
	2202 (0-6-0)		7700	2129	18000 (GT)
				2138	18100 (GT)
TOTAL 91					

By 1964, Swindon Works was a very different place. The Kings of course had gone, and the Castles were well on the way. And the works was now overhauling ex LMS Stanier and Ivatt 2-6- 0s. The 'New build' work comprised class 14 diesels. Little did we know that they were to have a very short lifespan. Western diesel hydraulics were well in evidence. Three on shed and thirteen on works.

Locomotive Performance website

B.R. Baterfield's Locomotive Records, 1964
SWINDON SHED & STOCK SHED (82C)

5060 Earl of Berkeley	5934 Kneller Hall
5074 Hampden	5955 Garth Hall
7005 Sir Edward Elgar	5963 Wimpole Hall
	6900 Abney Hall
1000 County of Middlesex	7902 Eaton Mascot Hall
1010 County of Carnarvon	7914 Lleweni Hall
1012 County of Denbigh	7916 Mobberley Hall
1014 County of Glamorgan	7926 Willey Hall
4916 Crumlin Hall	6804 Brockington Grange
4919 Donnington Hall	6873 Caradoc Grange
D1031 Western Rifleman	D826 Jupiter
D1041 Western Prince	D843 Sharpshooter
D1073 Western Bulwark	D864 Zambesi

6379 (2-6-0)	6130 (2-6-2T)	9605 (0-6-0T)	42760 (2-6-0)	D7004 Hymek	15100
		9680		D7009	
2244 (0-6-0)	4569 (2-6-2T)	9790	43940 (0-6-0)	D7064	D3512
	4591	44135			D9505
7221 (2-8-2T)		1658 (0-6-0T)		D4115	
	3677 (0-6-0T)	1664	D1717 (brush)	D4119	D2086
6106 (2-6-2T)	3702			D4120	D2146
6122	4626	W21 (Railcar)	D6915 (EE3)	D4122	
	7782		D6896	D4124	
TOTAL 62					

SWINDON LOCOMOTIVE WORKS & YARDS

5988 Bostock Hall	D1007 Western Talisman
6951 Impney Hall	D1009 Western Invader
6976 Graythwaite Hall	D1012 Western Firebrand
7924 Thorneycroft Hall	D1017 Western Warrior
7929 Wyke Hall	D1021 Western Sentinel
	D1027 Western Lancer
6823 Oakley Grange	D1035 Western Yeoman
6853 Morehampton Grange	D1036 Western Emperor
6862 Derwent Grange	D1047 Western Lord
	D1050 Western Ruler
7802 Bradley Manor	D1061 Western Envoy
7803 Barcote Manor	D1066 Western Prefect
	D1071 Western Renown
D837 Ramilles	
D850 Swift	D602 Bullog

92223 (2-10-0)	76075 (2-6-0)	8102 (2-6-2T)	4699 (0-6-0T)	D9509	D9521
	76076			D9511	
73034 (4-6-0)		8466 (0-6-0T)	D6828 (EE3)	D9512	D3026
	43001 (2-6-0)	8497		D9513	D3029
2818 (2-8-0)	43115	9425	D7004 Hymek	D9515	D3032
	43120	9457	D7008	D9516	D3754
42945 (2-6-0)	43137		D7011	D9517	D3824
42954		4600 (0-6-0T)		D9518	
42975	2210 (0-6-0)	4659	D9506	D9519	PWM 653
42978		4698	D9508	D9520	
TOTAL 72					

Diesels Made in Swindon

Western (BR Class 52) Diesel-Hydraulic Locomotives

Class:	52 (based on a German design, the Krauss-Maffei ML3000
Built:	British Rail 1961–1964
Engine:	Maybach 1,350hp × 2 (total of 2,700hp)
Transmission:	Hydraulic (in this choice of transmission Western Region stood alone against diesel–electric transmission)
Wheels:	C–C
Design Speed:	90mph.

Numbered in BR's original diesel serial number system

Built at Swindon Works

Number	Name	Number	Name
D1000	Western Enterprise	D1016	Western Gladiator
D1001	Western Pathfinder	D1017	Western Warrior
D1002	Western Explorer	D1018	Western Buccaneer
D1003	Western Pioneer	D1019	Western Challenger
D1004	Western Crusader	D1020	Western Hero
D1005	Western Venturer	D1021	Western Cavalier
D1006	Western Stalwart	D1022	Western Sentinel
D1007	Western Talisman	D1023	Western Fusilier
D1008	Western Harrier	D1024	Western Huntsman
D1009	Western Invader	D1025	Western Guardsman
D1010	Western Campaigner	D1026	Western Centurion
D1011	Western Thunderer	D1027	Western Lancer
D1012	Western Firebrand	D1028	Western Hussar
D1013	Western Ranger	D1029	Western Legionnaire
D1014	Western Leviathan		
D1015	Western Champion		

The Offices

The first offices built at the Works were on two floors at either end of the 1841 General Stores. The first known GWR personnel who had designated offices at the beginning of the Works in this building were, at the south end, T.H. Bertram, Engineer Swindon to Paddington District (and Chief Assistant I.K. Brunel. Bertram's name appears on many drawings regarding the Works) and a smaller office next door for Mr Owen, Superintendent of the line from Swindon to Box Tunnel. The other, of course, was Daniel Gooch, Locomotive Superintendent, who had a drawing office beside a model office and a rest room for when he stayed over at Swindon, these at the northern end of the building. Underneath Gooch's offices were ground floor offices for the accounts, the Stores' Keeper and reception area, whilst the ground floor at the southern end consisted of a Watchman's office, a mess room, and a bedroom and bathroom for Enginemen who had to stay over.

From these small beginnings grew a clerical empire housed in offices spread all around the Works that were squeezed in, converted, relocated, and, sometimes, even purpose-built:

These [locomotive works] are situated to the north of the main line, and are approached by a subway. At the end of the subway are the Locomotive Superintendent's Offices, a three-storeyed building of stone, having two wings 180 feet by 46 feet 6 inches and 148 feet by 45 feet 6 inches. This block also accommodates the Stores Superintendent and his staff.

Drawing Office. — This forms the top storey and consists of two wings 148 feet by 46 feet 6 inches and 148 feet by 45 feet 6 inches. It is one of the most up-to-date in the country, spacious and lofty, and lighted by inverted arc-lamps. In connection with the Drawing Office there is a large studio for photo-printing and photography built over part of an adjacent shop and having an outside south balcony, thus ensuring the best possible light.

Report on visit by the Institution of Mechanical Engineers,
The Engineer, 1908

Originally identified by name, i.e. Locomotive Superintendent's office, Works' Manager's office, Gas Work's Manager's office, Carriage Accountant's office, Time and Cash Office, they became so numerous that, just like the shops, the individual offices eventually had identifying numbers that changed and changed again through re-organisation and relocation over the decades.

Offices were also hierarchical. 'Shop' offices were the end of scale. Main offices were the 'hallowed halls'. The Drawing Office was for the 'chosen few.'

At one time, circa 1893, there were, in fact, several drawing offices.

Conrad Knowle Dumas:

The principal one, commonly called 'Dean's Drawing Office', was devoted to the design of locomotives and occupied the site immediately underneath the rolling stock section of the present Drawing Office. The storey which forms the latter did not exist.

There were Drawing Offices in both the Carriage and Wagon Works respectively. In the Loco Works there were two Drawing Offices, one devoted to building (commonly called 'the Building Office') and one (called 'the Loco Works Drawing Office') to the design of general machinery. The former had nothing to do with the Locomotive Works and was situated in their offices merely as a matter of convenience. It came under the same chief as 'Dean's Drawing Office', who was called 'the Chief Draughtsman'. The head of the 'Loco Works Drawing Office' was also foreman of the Test House. He had a separate private office, but the Chief Draughtsman had not. At one time draughtsmen in the Loco Works Office used to come to work at 6 a.m., but that had been done away with by my time.

Around 1900 all these separate Drawing Offices were amalgamated under one Chief Draughtsman. The Chief Draughtsman at that time, Mr H C King, had been Chief Inspector of Material and still retained that post. He was also given control of the Test House. The new office was housed in what is now the Fire Engine Station pending the building of the present office.

FASCINATING FACTS AND FIGURES

A Works memo for 16 December 1895 regarding recruitment of 'Additional Staff for Swindon' gives further information on the offices of that period. According to the list there were the:

District Loco & Carriage Superintendent's Office
Works' Manager's Office
Gas Works' Manager's Office
Carriage Accountant's Office
Chief Loco Superintendent's Office

All required extra clerks.

Prior to the 1950s all the offices had operated under the jurisdiction of the Locomotive Superintendent/CME and the heads of the departments would have been his 'assistants', but the BR management structure re-organisation placed the clerical staff under five separate autonomous departments, all of which needed separate office space.

Mechanical and Electrical Engineer (R.A. Smeddle)
Carriage and Wagon Engineer (C.T. Roberts)
Motive Power Superintendent (W.N. Pellow)
Stores Superintendent (H.R. Webb)
Chief Accountant (H.W. Gardner)

Office space was a continuing headache, especially through the 1960s–70s as the need to meet Government requirements in office accommodation (which they totally did not) became more pressing. Eventually the regimented 'classroom' rows of desks gave way to a more integrated open-plan office space. As the Works contracted so did the clerical workforce and the need for 'the offices'.

DID YOU KNOW?

Hats

Headwear carried its own significance in the Works and in society in New Swindon. There was a hierarchy in hats just as there was in every other part of their lives. The nature of one's hat denoted one's status and all the world could read it at a glance.

VIPs: homberg, bowlers and trilbies show the status of these men. Ted Plaister, head foreman of A Shop, sits proudly centre stage. From left to right, back: Foreman Wally Dew, Mr Raven AM Shop, ? , Foreman Millard. Front: Foreman Boilershop, ? , Ted Plaister, ? , Chargeman P1 Shop.

Flat Caps were worn by the shop floor men in and outside of work.

Trilby for the under-foreman.

Bowler hats were for the men-of-power on the shop floor – the foremen.

Hombergs for senior foremen or office managers.

Boaters and **Bonnets** meant holidays, Works' Outings and Fetes – hurrah.

Apprentice boys – and everybody capped!

Clerks

'Clerkdom' was a new opportunity born of the Industrial Revolution. The huge growth of 'paperwork' created by new business created a need for a new breed of worker – the clerk. It was a growth industry and as the railways expanded, so did the numbers of railway clerks employed. Being a 'railway clerk' was something 'other' to the general run-of-the-mill clerkdom in that they had a very specialised knowledge, which was not considered a 'transferable skill'.

Being 'a clerk' was an aspirational job that carried a certain status not just in the workplace but also in society at large. It was a somewhat misplaced conception of what being a clerk really was, especially a railway clerk. Only the very few made it to the top ranks of 'Chief Clerk' or 'Special Grades'. The phrase 'I am a lowly clerk' was not in common usage without reason. Nevertheless many aspired to make it to a '9 o'clock' post.

Aspiring young gentlemen, white-collar workers, hoping to make it up the clerical ladder – clerks in the Carriage Works c. 19??. H. Millard centre.

In early times most clerks, and again especially railway clerks, and especially shop-clerks, were not just overworked and generally poorly paid, they oft-times worked in difficult or horrendous situations. Even in the 1950s and '60s the Works were still struggling to meet legal requirements for appropriate working conditions for the clerical staff.

As with everything in the Works there was a hierarchy. 'Clerks' were linked with 'Officers' as it was 'white collar' work (indeed the stiff white collar was definitely the mode of dress for early clerks), rather than to the 'shopmen'. 'Clerk' was a 'graded' occupation. Women had a separate, limited grading to men during GWR times. British Rail grading went from 5 to 1 then 'Specials'. The 'in-joke' was 'Why am I only a Grade 5?' Response 'Because there are no Grade 6s!' Few men made it to Grade 3 and even fewer made it higher. After 1955 there was a re-organisation of the grading system and everyone started from Grade 4.

On application one had to take an examination. To progress one had to take the Senior Clerk's examination. Promotions came slowly, there was a lot of sideways movement, and there was a lot of waiting for dead men's shoes.

Great Western Railway
Locomotive Carriage & Wagon Department

STATEMENT OF THE TOTAL NUMBER OF OFFICERS, CLERKS AND DRAUGHTSMEN ON THE REGISTERED STAFF AS ON 12 SEPTEMBER 1911

Office	Authorised Staff 31/3/11	Authorised Staff 30/9/11
SWINDON		
Officers	25	25
Draughtsmen, etc.	48	49
Record	7	7
Statistical & Staff	10	10
Stationery	2	1
Running	46	46

Loco Accounts	134	136
Loco Factory Managers	31	31
Carriage & Wagon Accounts	56	56
C & W Stock	7	7
C & W Factory Managers	25	24
Timber Accounts	6	6
Superintendent & Assistants	3	3
Clerks	22	22

Signed C.J. Churchward

A British Railway Clerical Career Path
Ken Tanner:
Started 25 April 1949 – aged 15 years
15 Shop – C & W Works – *Office Boy*
Joined the GWR Superannuated Pension Scheme
National Service – aged 18 years
Return to Works aged 20
– Manager's Office – *Grade 5*
January 1955 Re-grading –
no more Grade 5s – new lowest *Grade 4* includes pay increase
1957 – Coaching Stock Records, C & W – *Grade 3*
1961 Staff Office – *Grade 3*
duties included working at the Booking Office in tunnel
Moved to Budgets and Internal Promotions – *Grade 3*
1970 – Training Section – *Grade 2*
1972 – Salaried Staff Section – *Special Grade*
Personnel Officer – 1986 Closure
Seconded to Great Western Enterprise
40 years' service – full pension benefits.

Female Clerks
Female clerks had been in the Works prior to the First World War, although in small numbers:

FASCINATING FACTS AND FIGURES

Miss Minnie Violet Southwell – a GWR female clerk:

D.O.B: 19 February 1895,
Position: Clerk (2)
Place: Marlowe House, Swindon
Started: 28 December 1910,
Age: 15 years.
Pay: 8/- per week.

✧ Left to be married 27 April 1935 (received Company's £10 Marriage Allowance)
✧ Re-entered Company Service May 1940 (war recruit) (now *Mrs* Jim Plaister)
✧ Temporary Clerk (2)
✧ Resigned with permission June 1943 [everyone had to have 'Official' permission to resign during the war]
✧ Re-entered December 1943
✧ Part-time clerk – 60/- per week
✧ Resigned February 1944 as required by Company on reaching 50 years of age.
✧ Work record – 34 years

The Mileage Office, 1923. One of the 'female-only' offices in the Works.

During the First World War significant numbers of young women were taken on as 'female clerks'. Some were to temporarily replace the men who had gone to war, the others were necessary to cope with the huge amount of extra work generated by the railways' war effort. The 'white blouse brigade' caused a great deal of consternation and fear for their jobs in the men. The employment was only for 'spinsters' and after application they had to wait to be sent for, wait until someone left to get married. For their 'moral welfare' and any 'inappropriateness' they were kept as separated from the men as was possible.

More women arrived during the Second World War, including *married* women, and, because of 'manpower' problems post-war, the Marriage Bar became more relaxed until it was no longer enforced. Offices eventually became more integrated with both men and women together – what would the GWR have thought about that?

Clerks: What Did They Do?

Clerks are the 'Cinderellas' of the railway world. Theirs was the unromantic but necessary 'housekeeping' part of the railway business but, as such, has attracted little attention. Few, unless they worked there, have any notion of what they actually did apart from the Wages Section, which was of vital importance to all the workers.

With other workers that worked 'Inside' what they did is fairly obvious – they created engines, built carriages, made wagons, produced parts, gas or oil, shunted, gave out or stored commodities, broke things up, moved things around – but clerks? The fact is that 'clerkdom' covered every aspect, no matter how minute, of what it took to run a railway company. For this vast amount of work you needed 'pen-pushers' as, before the age of typewriters and computers, everything (almost) was handwritten.

To cover such work in this book would be impossible but here, via the Works' Telephone Exchange extension numbers, is a small insight into the different areas of work involved in two sections in 1962:

Clerical Offices (General)

2060	Head of Section
2054	Contracts & Orders – Clerk-in-Charge
2055	Contracts (Electrical) & New Works & Sundry Orders
2734	Correspondence Registration
2061	Records – Machinery, Cranes, Agreements, B.S.S. etc.
2060	Suggestions, Works Visits, Claims, etc.
2070	Main Works Entrance
2069	Messengers

Purchasing Sections

2483	'A' Section, Head Of Section
2479	'A' Section, General
2487	'B' Section, Head of Section: Timber, Fly, Block and Hardboard, Plastic Sheet
2477	'B' Section, Permanent Way Materials
2481	'B' Section, Permanent Way Materials – Progressing, Building Materials
2491	'B' Section, Electrical, Signal & Telegraph Materials

And in the 'Personnel Section' during the much reduced BREL era:

Personnel and Administration
Personnel and Administration Officer   077-2007
     Management by Objectives Office   077-2027
     Staff Officer   077-2009
     Clerical Section:
         Section Leader – Wages Staff   077-2293
         Statistics and Recruitment   077-2299
         Records, Sickness, Annual Leave   077-2294
         Accidents and Protective Clothing   077-2076
         Section Leader – Salaried Staff   077-2291
         Travel Facilities, Timekeeping, Leave 077-2292
         Stationary and Reprographics   077-2734
         Training and M by O   077-2274
         Secretary and Dining Hall   077-2159
         Training Officer   077-2008
         Training Assistant (Manual Skills) 077-2499
         Training Assistant (Salaried Staff) 077-2499

Job description
Howard Jones:

I was a lowly railway clerk, a small cog in a very big wheel. When I became secretary of the GWR Loco & Carriage Dept. Sick Fund Society, commonly known as the Yard Club, one of the jobs was to look in the Adver and see if there was any recorded deaths. Well the new boss came in he saw me reading the Adver, he didn't say anything, he went in his office and called Stan Green who was the Section Leader and wanted to know why he was letting someone read the Adver in full view of everyone else and he was told in no uncertain terms that it was part of my job to look for deaths of members of the Society.

Such was the minutiae of railway life.

DID YOU KNOW?

The Check and 'the Checkie'

'Checkie' was a name that was feared, hated or loved, as he was the man who 'checked' the men into work. He had the power to 'make you late' by shutting the check-board dead on time with your check still hanging there, and thereby lose money, or being helpful and giving you a minute or so grace.

GWR Rule 8 (1875) explains:

> Each workman is furnished with a brass ticket [known as 'the check'] having his number stamped on it which he must himself deposit in the box appointed for the purpose every time he returns to his work. If he neglects to do this he will be paid half-time only for that particular portion of the day.
>
> If any man deposits the ticket of another workman he will be discharged immediately and the man who requests or allows another workman to deposit his ticket, will be dealt with in the same way.

The 'checks' were hung on a board in each shop known as 'the check-board'. The GWR's magazine described it as, 'Like a show-case with rows of small hooks and with a front glass panel that slides upwards to open.' This was manned by 'the checkie'.

The warning bell would ring (later it was the Hooter that would blow) and then the men who failed to check-in exactly on time, each time, would lose a quarter of an hour's pay. In later years, the 'checkie' played a 'policing' role. Apprentices starting in a new shop had to report to the checkie to be allocated their new 'check' for that shop. Percy Warwick remembers, 'When I went in there first in 1939, under a certain age the starting time was later than the usual and I can always remember the checkie coming up to me the night before my birthday saying, 'You'll be 15 tomorrow so tomorrow you start at 8 o'clock' and I had to start like the rest of the men.' The 'checkie' knew everyone and everything about everyone! It was this that made him a useful member of the shop and the reason behind the workshop slogan 'See the checkie, he'll see you right'.

Checks
Small metal disks punched with a hole, rounded bottomed for Loco-side but heart-shaped for C & W.

Red ones denoted 'absence' ¼ and ½ denoted time 'lost' and not paid 'see the foreman' was not what you wanted to see – it meant you had been late too often!

3
MYTHS AND LEGENDS

The 'Legend'

The romantic story of how the Works began suggests that the site of the Works was decided 'on the toss of a sandwich', which was purportedly part of the picnic lunch of Isambard Kingdom Brunel and Daniel Gooch, Brunel's assistant. It tells that they said where the sandwich fell determined where the new factory would rise. Fun, but nonsense!

LETTERS OR NUMBERS?

Everything in the factory had a letter or number. At the beginning the buildings were given names and letters, such as B shed. With new buildings and alterations the names and letters were altered and adjusted a great many times over the years.

1875

Circular

20 July 1875

In consequence of the erection of the new shops on the S/west side of the Works, several alterations and additions to the initial letters of various shops will be necessary, the following will, therefore, in future be the letters for Shops mentioned below. Please give instructions for the changes for them, to be made accordingly –

Millwright (old Boiler Shop)	G
New Copp. Smith Shop (old Tender shop)	K
New tender shop & Machine Shop	P
--- Smithy will remain	Q
New Brass Finishers Shop (including Gas Fitters and Locksmiths)	T
New Brass Foundry	U
New Boiler Shop & Machine shop	V

Signed J. Carlton

All Foremen .

The Machine shops adjt the Boiler & Tender Shops will be lettered P & V respectively the same as the shops with which they are connected.

1935

The Locomotive Works' shops had **LETTERS**

A	Erectors, Boilermakers, Painters, Machine and Wheel Shop
B	Erectors, Boilermakers, Painters and Tender Shop
C	Concentration Yard
D1	Carpenters
D2	Masons'Yard
E	Electrical Shop
F and F2	Smiths, Springsmiths and Chainmakers
G	Millwrights
H	Pattern Makers
J	Iron Foundry
J2	Chair Foundry
K	Coppersmiths and Sheet Metal Workers
L2	Tank Shop
M	Electric Sub-Station
N	Bolt Shop
O	Tool Room
P1	Steaming and Boiler Mounting

P.L	Locomotive Works, Platelayers, Rails, Roads and Water Mains Maintenance
Q	Angle Iron Smiths
R	Fitters, Turners and Machinemen
SP	Springsmiths
T	Brass Finishers
TH	Testing House
U	Brass Foundry
V	Boilermakers
W	Turners and Machinemen
X	Points and Crossings Fittings for Permanent Way

But with the coming of the Carriage & Wagon Works **NUMBERS** came into play

1	Sawmill (West End)
2	Sawmill
3	Fitting and Machines
4	Carriage Body Building
5	Electric Train Lighting Equipment
6	Carriage Body Repairs
7	Carriage Finishing
8	Carriage Painting
9	Carriage Trimming
9a	Lining Sewers (Female)
10	Laundry (Female)
10a	Polishers (Female)
11	General Labourers
12	Carpenters
I2a	Polishers
13	Wagon Frame Building
13a	Carriage Frame Repairs
14	Smiths
15	Fitting and Machines
15a	Plumbers, Gas and Steam Fitters, Tinmen and Coppersmiths
16	Wheel
16a	Case-hardening and Normalizing

17	Road Vehicle Building and Repairing
18	Stamping
19	Carriage Repairs (subdivided as under)
19a	Carriage Trimmers Repairs
19b	Carriage Finishers Repairs
19c	Carriage Lifters
19d	Vacuum Brake and Carriage Bogie Repairs
20	Horse Box and Carriage and Truck Repairs
21	Wagon Building and Repairs, Wood Section
21a	Wagon Repairs, Iron Section
21b	Wagon Painting
22	Oil and Grease Works
23	Platelayers' Yard, Maintenance and Breaking-up Yard
24	Carriage Paint Repairs
24a	Carriage Body Repairs

1950

Now British Railways – Spot the Difference – Letters and Numbers

Shops in the Locomotive Works:

Shop	Description
A	Erectors, Boilermakers, Painters, Machine and Wheel Shop
B	Erectors, Boilermakers, Painters and Tender Shop
BSE	Engine Reception and Preparation
C	Concentration Yard (recovery of scrap metal)
D	Carpenters and Masons
E	Electrical Shop
F	Smiths, Springsmiths and Chainmakers
G	Millwrights
H	Pattern makers
J	Iron Foundry
J2	Chair Foundry
K	Coppersmiths and Sheet Metal Workers
L2	Tank Shop
M	Electric Sub-Station
N	Bolt Shop

O	Tool Room
P1	Steaming and Boiler Mounting
PL	Platelayers, Loco. Works, Rails, Roads and Water Mains Maintenance
Q	Angle Iron Smiths
R	Fitters, Turners and Machinemen
SP	Springsmiths
T	Brass finishers
TH	Testing House
U	Brass Foundry
V	Boilermakers
W	Turners and Machinemen
X	Points and Crossings, Fittings for Permanent Way
Z	Transport

Shops in the Carriage & Wagon Works

Shop	Description
1	Sawmill (West End)
2	Sawmill
3	Fitting and Machines
4	Carriage Body Building
5	Electric Train Lighting
7	Carriage Finishing and Polishers
8	Carriage Painting
9	Carriage Trimming
9a	Lining Sewers (female)
10	Laundry (female)
11	General Labourers
12	Carpenters
13	Wagon Frame Building
13a	Carriage Frame Repairs
14	Smiths
15	Fitting, Machining, Plumbers, Gas and Steam Fitters, Sheet Metal Workers and Coppersmiths
16	Wheel
17	Road Vehicle Building and Repairing

18	Stamping
19a	Carriage Trimmers Repairs
19b	Carriage Finishers Repairs
19c	Carriage Lifters
19d	Vacuum Brake and Carriage Bogie Repairs
20	Horse Box and Carriage Truck Repairs
21	Wagon Building and Repairs
22	Oil and Grease Works
23	Platelayers' Yard, Maintenance and Breaking-up Yard
24	Carriage Repairs

1972

Now BREL – a much contracted Swindon Works – ALL shops are NUMBERED

Workshop No	Designation
1	Train Heating Shop
2	Transmission Shop
3	Machine and Fitting Shop
4	Copper and Sheet Metal Shop
5	Diesel Locomotive Repair Shop (inc. O D M & C C E equipment repair section)
6	Electric Traction Shop
7	Loco Bogie, Wheel and Final Drive Shop
8	Diesel Testing Station
9	Diesel Engine Repair Shop
10	Foundry, Pattern and Whitemetal Shop
11	Brake Equipment Shop
12	Wagon and Container Repair Shop
13	Steel Fabrication Shop
14	B R U T E Shop
15	Smiths and Butt Welding Shop
16	Heat Treatment Shop
17	Wire Rope and Chain Test House
18	Spring Shop
19	Diesel Multiple Unit Repair Shop (inc. Battery Shop)

20	C & W Bogie Wheel and Final Drive Shop
21	Steel Preparation and Paint Spray (formerly loco reception)
32	Tool Room
33	Mechanical Maintenance Shop (inc. Maintenance Garage)
34	Building Maintenance
35	Electrical Maintenance Shop
36	Fire Station and Workshop (inc. Laboratory & Diesel Training School)
37	Scrap Recovery (inc. incinerators)
53	Yard and General Labourers
54	Works Transport Garage

1981

No	Designation
Production Shops	
3	Machine
4	Coppersmith/S Metal Workers, Welders
6	Electrical
9	Engines & Transmissions
10	Foundry & Non-ferrous
11	Brakes
12	Wagons
13B	Weld/Fab – Machines
14	BRU Trollies
15/16	Blacksmiths/Heat Treatment
18	Springs
19/19A	DMU, EMU & Non Pass
20	Wheel
21	Asbestos House
24	White Metal
25	Locomotives

B & Q Service Shops

8	Diesel Test Station
13A	Welding & Fabrication
17	Wire Rope/Chain Testing
22	C C E
32	Tool Room
33	Mechanical Maintenance
34	Building Maintenance
35	Electrical Maintenance
36	Fire Brigade
37	Scrap Recovery
38	Pattern Makers
39	Maintenance Garage
45	Boiler Stations
52	Security
53/54	Transport/Yard Labour
71	Stores

DID YOU KNOW?

Toilets

G. W. R.
NOTICE.
WORKMEN'S LAVATORY.
WORKMEN USING THIS CLOSET MUST ON ENTERING
GIVE THEIR TICKET NUMBERS TO THE ATTENDANT.
IF LONGER TIME THAN TEN MINUTES IS TAKEN
THE WHOLE TIME WILL BE STOPPED.
APRIL 1904.   BY ORDER.

Did you know that the workmen's toilet breaks were timed but the foremen had special treatment, having their own toilets and keys?

Workshops: Early Beginnings and Dying Moments. These pictures are both by Works employees. The top one was reproduced in *The Illustrated Exhibitor* 1852 and the bottom one was taken by Andy Binks in 1986, as the shops were cleared for closure. The Works had fought steam and diesel for its existence through one economic crisis to another; it was finally done to death by those whose loyalties and sympathies lay elsewhere.

ONE BIG 'FAMILY'

If anything has and deserves legend status it is that Swindon Works' workers, Loco or Carriage & Wagon, in the offices or in the stores, labourers, shunters, steam and diesel, all talk of themselves as 'one big family'. It is more than a feeling, more than whole families generation after generation putting-in-the-time; it is an *esprit de corps* as cited by Richard Jeffries (1875) but more than that it is a shared experience, a shared caring and a shared responsibility that goes back even to its earliest times as this piece so clearly demonstrates:

> The Great Western Railway Company have felt the need of reducing the expenditure at their factory, and a great number of labourers have been discharged from Swindon Works. Orders were received to discharge 400 of the men, but the foremen of the different shops, held a meeting at which it was resolved to consent that the whole body should work short-time instead of so many hands being turned adrift at a time when they would have difficulty in procuring employment,
>
> The hands, therefore, at the factory now only work four days a week instead of six.
>
> *Devizes and Wiltshire Gazette*, Thursday 4 November 1847

A century later **Arthur Jell** tells how he ended up as part of that 'big Works family' after his demob from the Armed Services in the late 1940s:

> I went to the Labour Exchange. I said 'Are there any jobs going in the factory, Inside, like?' He said, 'what do you want to do in there, then?' I said, 'Anything.' When I got in there I thought this will do me for a fortnight to see how it was, but I ended up spending thirty eight years in there. Once you went in there, you were in there for life. I was sixty four plus when I finished. I enjoyed going to work. It wasn't the money, because that wasn't very good. It was because of the attitude in there. Just a factory but *it was like a family*.

Ryan Conduit experienced the same feelings decades later in the 1980s:

> You had to know the people who worked there. I can say that the people I worked with, they were not work mates, they felt more than that. It was like a family in a way. I have tried over the years to recapture the feeling I had working there, I know that I never ever will.

Folklore has it that those born into Great Western Railway families came with the initials GWR stamped on their bottoms – and for Swindon people, maybe SWINDON WORKS on their foreheads. This held true even when GWR ceased to exist and the Works was under British Rail, even until the Works' closure – under their skin these people were Swindon Works through and through. Many family histories verify this statement – some, maybe surprisingly, include railway women.

My Family Tree

The Dyer family came originally from Bath and Hungerford. Theirs is a fascinating history from the earliest times of the Works, highlighting not only the rising status of the family but also the changing nature of work undertaken 'Inside'.

Richard Dyer, 1842–1861, Father

1842–1843	Porter Swindon Station (joined aged 39 years)
1843–1861	Labourer Locomotive Works

Richard Llewllyn Dyer, 1851–1911, son

Richard Dyer was a popular Foreman who looked after the welfare of his men and his retirement presentation was a notable occasion and duly written up in the Company's records and magazine.

1851–1854	Boy labourer
1854–859	Apprentice Boilermaker
1859–1866	Boilermaker
1866–1911	Foreman of Boilermaker's Department. (In 1866 when he took this position there were 130 men engaged in the trade, at his retirement there were 800.)

Horace Dyer, 1895–1933, grandson

1890–1895	Apprentice Fitter
1896–1906	Fitter
1906–1933	CME's Records & Patents Office

Roger Washington Dyer, 1930–1973, great-grandson

It is with Roger we seen the changing 'face' of the Works as it transfers from steam to diesel.

1930–1935	Apprentice
1936–1939	Fitter AM Shop
1939–1946	War Service
1946–1953	Foreman R Machine Shop
1954	Foreman Diesel Engine Repairs
1956	Foreman Diesel Engine Testing Station
1960	Chief Estimator Loco. Works
1964	Technical Costs Assistant Swindon Works
1966	Superintendent Engine & Transmission Repair Shops
1973	Took early retirement.

The Hadley Family connection goes back to the early GWR days when great grandfather George worked as an engine cleaner on the Broad Gauge engines in Farringdon Engine Shed, while George's brother Joseph, came to Swindon Works.

Their women joined the tradition in clerical work. What stands out is Uncle Frank, the lone Loco man in a family of C & W men!

Relationship	Name	Date in Works	Occupation	Place
Great Uncle	Joseph	unknown	unknown	Works
Grandfather	Richard Henry	1896–1925	carpenter	C & W
Father	Richard E George	1911–1962	wagon builder	C & W
Uncle	Francis (Frank)	1913–1964	boiler-mate	Loco
Uncle	Herbert Reginald	1915–1966	wagon builder	C & W
Uncle	William Cyril OBE	1929–1978	metal machinist	C & W
	Eric	1942–1986	coach builder	C & W
Twin brother	Clifford	1942–1984	plumber	C & W
Sister	Elsie	1945–1952	clerk	Offices
	Ernest Henry	1938–1985	carpenter	C & W
	Hazel	1953–1960	clerk	Offices
	Michael C	1947–1980	clerk	C & W
	Margaret	1984–1986	clerk	offices

This amazing record was disturbed only by military service.

Both sexes of **the Pinnegar family** worked 'Inside' and in the factory and on 'railway work proper' (to use Railway Commentator Edwin Pratt's phrase).

Albert John Pinnegar – 1910 to 1965 – father
Holder-up who worked his whole time in Loco V Boiler Shop. His job was to work inside the engine's boiler and hold up his hammer to the red hot rivet while it was riveted with a pneumatic riveter from the outside. The incessant noise left many boilermakers stone deaf in later years.

Gordon Pinnegar – 1934 to 1979 – brother
Boilermaker Loco V Boiler Shop.

Ken Pinnegar – 1938 to 1982 – brother
Blacksmith welder F2 Shop.

Derrick Pinnegar – brother
Machinist Loco AE Shop.

Mrs Pamela Rose Arthurs (nee Pinnegar) 1947 to 1953 – daughter
One of the rare women recruited directly into 'railway work proper' *not* in the war years, but came through a 'family connection'. Hammer driver, F Shop Loco Works. Worked with Blacksmiths on small 5cwt steam hammers making locomotive fittings and hand tools.

Peggy Pinnegar – 1949 to 1952 – daughter
Hammer Driver F Shop – another of those 'rare' not war-recruited female railway workers.

Malcom Pinnegar – nephew?

Albert Francis Arthurs – 1936 to 1980 – husband of Peggy
Hammer Driver – Striker
F Shop and Steam Hammer Shop.

Throughout the decades such family trees were common.

Frederick 'Fred' Griffin:
All his family were in there at one time.
His father worked in there.

His mother had also worked in there.
Three brothers all worked in there.
Three sisters too, all doing French polishing.

Rob Deejay Simpkins:
> Me, my sister, my Dad, he was a fitter, all of his brothers and his Dad my Grandad a boiler maker like me, all worked Inside. That's pretty iconic in itself I think.

Fred Bradbury was an apprentice at Swindon Works from 1960 to early 1966 in the trade of coach painting and signwriting. His family had a long association with the Works over many years and in a variety of trades. His elder brother was a carpenter and joiner; his father was in the tinsmith's shop; and his grandfather was a pattern maker. This range of trades is somewhat unusual in that the tradition of the Works was that son follows father into their trade.

Mrs Nora Hunt:
> My father became a roof canvaser on coaches and insulated meat wagons … my brother, born 1900, became the youngest foreman in the railway as oil tester and inspector at the Oil and Grease Works. … My sister became a clerk in the General Manager's office. … I had an uncle who worked in the Brass Foundry. … My sister's husband was a fitter and turner … my sister-in-law's husband was a wonderful cabinet maker and wood artist. My contribution came in 1927 when at sixteen I entered the railway company as a shorthand typist in the Chief Accountant's Audit Office. We were a family who helped to run 'God's Wonderful Railway' so that all could share This England.

'THE HOOTER'

If there is one thing that identifies Swindon Works it is 'the Hooter'. The Hooter went with the Works and Swindon Town like bacon and eggs, fish and chips, or Brunel and the GWR. It was (and is in memory) much loved. It was a Swindon 'treasure'.

The Hooter was part and parcel of everyday life, whether you worked 'Inside' or not and, like the Works, it had a chequered life. It brought the wrath of the local lord down on its head, and it united the workforce and Swindonians in its defence.

In the days before everyone had a clock or watch, the Hooter was 'the time' people lived their lives by, got up by, had their meals prepared and ready by, and, more importantly, the chance to arrive at work 'on time' and avoid having their pay docked.

The 'Hooter' started life as 'a large bell' fixed to the roof of C shed, became a 'whistle' (or 'steam trumpet' as it was sometimes called) mounted on the roof of the 1864 Fitting and Machine Shop, over its steam engine power house, and then became and remained – a 'Hooter' on the Central Power Station or 'Hooter House'.

August 1857

NOTICE

In addition to the present system of ringing the bell for summoning the workmen, it will in future be rung a second time beginning 3 minutes before each hour, that is 5.57 am, 8.57 am and 1.57 pm, and continue ringing for a further 2 minutes. The door will be closed punctually at the hour and the special attention of all workmen is called to Rules 6 & 7.

Sgd W F Gooch

As the numbers of workmen grew and came from further afield, the need for the 'sound' to travel further became apparent and a 'whistle' was introduced.

March 19th 1869

Circular

On and after Wednesday the 31st inst., I have arranged for the Factory Whistle to be blown at 6.0am, 9.0am and 2.0 pm, so that no excuse can be made for men not commencing work at the right time.

Please inform your men of this and any person not commencing work at the proper time after this arrangement will be severely dealt with.

Sgd S Carlton

Hooter Times

At 5.20 a.m. for a period of 10 minutes
At 5.30 a.m. for a period of 3 minutes
At 6 a.m. for a period of 1 minute
At 8.15 a.m. for a period of 30 seconds
At 8.50 a.m. for a period of 30 seconds
At 9 a.m. for a period of 30 second
At 1 p.m. for a period of 30 seconds
At 1.50 p.m. for a period of 30 seconds
At 2 p.m. for a period of 30 seconds
At 6 p.m. for a period of 30 seconds

The initial 'blast' was early and for an extraordinarily long time, not to the liking of all, especially the local lord at Lydiard, three miles away. William Morris, in his book tells how Lord Bolingbroke …

'set up some sentimental personal grievance of his own against the convenience of some five or six thousand working men: when he objected to the use of a steam whistle for calling the thousands of workmen to their labours on the grounds that its noise might possibly frighten and disturb a few of his pheasants sitting on their eggs a few miles off.

Bolingbroke's application for the whistle to be stopped set off a real hullabaloo that sounded as loud and as far as the whistle itself! It became a 'battle of the classes', worker against gentry. To placate Bolingbroke the 'whistle' was changed and the timings shortened.

LORD BOLINGBROKE AND THE SWINDON HOOTER

*"Will any doctor or physician come forward and say
That the health of this gentleman is going to decay
Through the sound of a trumpet vibrating the air?
No, not one on his account will come, I declare."*

June 7th 1872

NOTICE

Commencing on Monday next the Factory Whistle will be taken down and a Locomotive Guard's Whistle fixed in its place. <u>Signed</u> S Carlton per E Riley

It was to no avail and the Local Board placed a sanction on its use under the Nuisances Removal Acts. So incensed were the workers and the townsfolk, they campaigned and called for a review. Hearing nothing they held their own meeting at 'the Mechanics'. Chairman of the Meeting, Mr W.R. Wearing, reported that they had been to see the Hon. F.W. Cadogan, MP for Cricklade (which then included Swindon) who had informed them that all they had to do was switch one hooter for another. Joseph Armstrong then announced that 'the Company was constructing a new hooter, not a steam whistle but an atmospheric one'. The Local Government Board eventually delivered its verdict on 7 July 1874 to: 'revoke the sanction to use such Steam Whistle or Steam Trumpet as from the First day of August 1874.'

Sometime later '*the* Hooter' (which was actually *two* hooters – one for near sound, the other for distant) was re-sited on the Central Power Station, at the north-east corner of the boiler shop; and became known locally as the 'Hooter House'. 'The Hooter' also reverted again to steam. An official 1892 Hooter drawing identifies it as such and it is this design that became a Swindon landmark, silhouetted proud against the skyline.

The Hooter was also used for other reasons, notably as an 'alarm' during war periods.

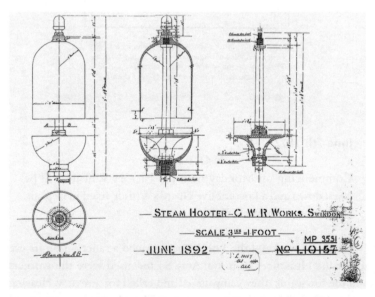

This magnificent technical drawing shows the exact dimensions and specifications of a new *steam* hooter, which it remained until the end. (David Hyde Collection)

SWINDON WORKS HOOTER				
MONDAY to THURSDAY			FRIDAY	
TIME	DURATION		TIME	DURATION
6·45	17 SECS		6·45	17 SECS
7·20	12 SECS		7·20	12 SECS
7·25	7 SECS		7·25	7 SECS
7·30	12 SECS		7·30	12 SECS
12·30	12 SECS		1·30	12 SECS
1·05	12 SECS			
1·10	7 SECS			
1·15	12 SECS			
4·30	12 SECS			

(MORNING for the first block; AFTERNOON for the second block)

NOTICE

The Hooter may be used at any hour for military signals and such signals will be given by a number of short blasts.

Please put this notice in your shop.

Ten blasts at 7.49 p.m. on 4 August 1914 announced the beginning of the First World War to Swindon and thereafter six short blasts announced 'an emergency.' During the Second World War it was again brought into 'military' action. In later years the blasts were of a shorter duration.

The Hooter was much loved in Swindon, especially by the 'Insiders'.

The Voice of the Works

There is really only one hooter. Other local industries have whistles, sirens ... some even boast hooters of their own; but their puny pipings bear no comparison with the full-throated bellow of the Works hooter carried on a westerly gale. Swindon would not be the same without the old hooter's clarion call.

Swindon Railway News, 1960

'Hooter Man' Arthur Davis operating the hooter at the Swindon Railway works on 27 August 1919.

Around this time the water capacity in the Works was reduced and the water tank against which the Hooter was fixed was dismantled. The Hooters were then fixed to the side of the building with an additional supporting rail. During this their height was lowered and the manner in which they 'blasted' changed. Cyril Godwin, then foreman of K Shop, remembers that at this time K Shop supplied new 2¼in pipes and that the controls changed from a ball valve to a tap valve, all of which had the effect of a slower start at a reduced pitch leading to a gradual build up to a full head of steam. The Hooter now slowly rumbled into effect rather than opening its lungs and blasting.

The last sounding of the Hooter heralded the final closing of the Works.

When 'the Hooter' blew for the last time 26 March 1986 at 4.30 p.m. it was a momentously sad moment for many Swindonians as years of history were carried away as steam and sound on the wind.

DID YOU KNOW?

'Funny Goings On'

'Funny goings on' is a phrase that was repeated many times by railway men and women to describe different experiences in the Works over many generations, that and 'what they got up to is nobody's business'. These 'going's on' were part of the culture and character of the Works.

There were many 'traditions' of 'pranks' against lads and young apprentices. The most commonly talked of was 'the stand and long weight.' Sent to the Stores or another part of the shop for a 'stand and long weight about five to ten' the lad, having made this request, would then be told to 'just stand over there for a mo while I deal with this will you' and after waiting patiently for some time, he would remind the man he was still there. 'Oh, how long have you been standing and waiting?' 'About five to ten minutes.' 'I think you've waited long enough then, don't you?' Penny drops. Laughs all round.

Nigel Hobbs:

In 6 shop we would 'tail' an apprentice with a long strip of blue paper towel, sometimes even lighting it. Sometimes apprentices went home looking like flour graders, totally covered in French chalk. How many of us carried around the 'happy slap' – white or pink handprints on the back of our overalls from the pink hand barrier cream?

Jim Toolen:

Remember having your heels painted with silver paint from someone down in the pits in the A shop and then the calling of 'Ye-haa!' as to the spurs you were wearing – extra brownie points if you got a chargehand!

Andy Binks, 1970s:

As an apprentice working in the BD Shop (later 9 Shop) life was always good fun. A lot of the chaps were quite young and you would enjoy many laughs during the working days. Usually on a Friday afternoon they would have various competitions. One was how many people you could get touching a turbo blower; this was a three foot round unit out of a diesel engine. The word would go round that they were going for the record and everybody had to stand with one finger touching a turbo. If memory served me correct I think the record was around seventy-six. Can you image, seventy six men, arms stretched out as far as possible, crammed around the turbo blower? Not something the Foreman would have encouraged much! If they weren't doing that, it was to see how many men they could fit into a chargeman's box. These were about 4' square, 7' high with a desk inside. The record I believe was into the twenties with some men and boys in some very compromising positions indeed!

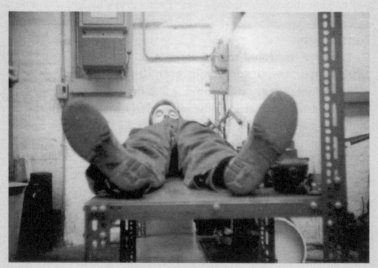

Another name for 'funny goings-on' was 'larking', much to the annoyance of the management. Bob Townsend does his best 'larking' here in the T Shop – or the Brass Shop – in 1962.

'FOREIGNERS'

What is a 'foreigner'? For most of us it means the same thing – *but* in Swindon Works it had a special meaning – something quite different.

Dictionary Definition:
a 'foreigner' *is a person not belonging to a particular place or group; a stranger or outsider; someone from another country.*

There were actually many of these in the Works, especially to begin with as the men with the necessary skills for the new engineering factory were not the indigent agricultural workers, but those from further afield mining towns. The 1851 Census shows that originally these families came from Scotland, Cumberland, Durham, Northumberland, Smithfield in London and several other places. Other notables are the Welsh who came up in large numbers to build and work the Rolling Mills in 1861 and built a 'little Wales' in Cambrai Place, too.

Alfred Williams mentions a number of 'foreigners' in the workshops – 'The men are a mixture of many sorts and of several nationalities – English [from Penzance] Scotch, Welsh and Irish.'

Then there were the women who came from London, Bristol and other centres for war-work during the First World War and those conscripted in the Second World War; also at that time the Italian prisoners-of-war (these divided themselves into two groups – the Fascists, who wore dark patches, and the 'friendlies', who called themselves Compatriots). They caused great consternation to the men as well as the women. The men found them interesting because of their very dark, well-shaped hair and the women found them exotic and exciting, so that much flirtation went on. The prisoners worked mostly at menial jobs such as general sweeping-up and raking out the quantities of ash from the locomotives in the Running Shed.

A little later in the 1950s and early '60s there was the influx of newly arrived Londoners, who were housed in the 'overspill' development at Walcot, Swindon, and during the same period the

Polish immigrants, who worked mainly in the 'hot-shops'. These were hard workers – keen workers, indeed much too keen for the local men. The Polish workers would find a way into the shops and have their fires hot and ready so that they could start production immediately the moment 'time' arrived.

Swindon Works Definition:

A 'foreigner' *is something that was made in the Works – but should not have been, i.e. it was for personal and private not Company use.*

Almost every Works' family would have had 'a foreigner' in their house. These could be anything from curtains made by the women in the Trimming Shop – Clive Wilson's Aunty Joan worked in the Sewing Shop: 'She would make us anything, curtains, cushions, tea towels, anything my mum needed' – to practical pokers and tongs or metal coal buckets for the fires in their homes, or ornamental vases and beautifully crafted metal flowers to put in them. Arthur Jell remembers 'foreigners' vividly: 'They would make their clothes lines in the Works. They would be boiler tubes – full length of the engine they were, and they would take them home on the corporation bus at night. They were all over Swindon. Still there now I expect. Joe Cook, he made his and took it on the bus. Just shoved it up the middle of the bus like. Nothing ever bothered that bloke, Joe Cook. He made his fork in work to use on his allotment.' One very popular 'foreigner' speciality was a brass 21st birthday key (when that was the age of adulthood) with your name or initials engraved on it. There were many of these made over the years. Legend has it that the biggest 'foreigner' made in the Works was a conservatory, which was brought out bit by bit, and rebuilt in 'someone's' back garden.

Philip Musty:

Yes, Friday afternoon particularly was often spent making 'foreigners' for various people – important part of our apprenticeship we were often told.

WOMEN

Many would perhaps be surprised to know women workers entered the factory *before* they entered the offices. The Works were finding it hard to recruit skilled men as they did not want to bring their families to the frontier town of New Swindon, there being little or no work for their daughters. Joseph Armstrong, Locomotive and Carriage & Wagon Superintendent, took a bold and radical step and decided to create a 'shop' just for 'the fair sex', as the GWR liked to call them – which was to be kept entirely separate from the men.

A letter in GWR Board Reports written by Joseph Armstrong states:

28 November 1871

A new Shop is required in Swindon for the employment of Female labour in working sewing machines, French polishing, Horse Hair dressing and other work in connection with carriage trimmings: additional accommodation is also required for Carriage painting and finishing.

A GWR register also shows that girls were employed in the Carriage Department from at least 1874 – if not earlier:

Alphabetical Register of Workmen CARRIAGE DEP:
Oct 1877–1907

Name	Entered	Left	Job
1874			
Mary Burge	15/08/74	13/11/80	Ling Wm
Cecilia Fullond	18/07/74	–	POL (earliest date)
Mary Isles	05/08/74	13/11/80	POL
Jessie McGregor	15/08/74	24/12/78	POL
Martha Ribson	15/12/74	23/12/80	POL
1875			
Caroline Shaw	03/11/75	01/07/87	POL
Isabella Turnbull	23/06/75	–	POL
Sarah Jane Sanders	16/07/75	10/10/78	POL
Harriet Smith	16/07/75	05/04/78	POL
Rachel Smith	13/08/75	12/04/90	POL
Ellen Dempsey	02/11/75	–	POL

Ling Wmn stood for lining woman, also recorded as a 'sewer', someone who sewed.

POL stood for polisher, i.e. French polisher, an artisan trade and therefore very surprising.

Polishing

Although polishing at home was women's work, French polishing was craft work, it required training and therefore was not for women. Yet, despite the fact that this was seen as 'temporary' employment between leaving school and woman's rightful destiny, marriage, the girls were taught how to 'pickle' and strip, colour and tone and finally polish and 'finish' anything that was made of wood in the train – doors, panels, window frames, luggage rack poles, wood partitions, even toilet seats!

The next time women made inroads into the workshops was during the First World War.

An official GWR drawing identified as 'lavatory accommodation for women Loco Works Swindon' dated October 1916 and written up as 'adopted', shows that toilet and canteen accommodation was instigated for female employees in the old K shop, which was the coppersmith's shop. Family histories also support the fact that women were taken on to do munitions work *and* 'railway' work such as carriage cleaning. One such was young Mrs Lily Mary Walter who cleaned carriages with Mrs Fluck, mother of Swindon celebrity Diana Dors, whilst Mrs Fanny Hyde and Miss Winnie Hyde left domestic service and were taken on at the Works to do munitions.

The Second World War saw another intake, this time doing a great deal of 'proper' railway work in many different workshops and in previously 'male-only' occupations. A perhaps surprising official list gives us insight into just what the women did:

A new breed of 'hammerman' – hammerwoman. War made challenging demands on the people, sending women into traditional 'male-only' territories. Second World War recruit Mrs Phyllis Saunders left her sewing job in a raincoat factory and was sent to work on this 20cwt hammer in the Blacksmith's. Only for the wartime, of course – it was thought, but some came back after the war and stayed until the mid-1950s.

Chief Mechanical Engineer's Department
SWINDON

Tues. 23 September 1941
Employment Of Women In Place Of Men

Conciliation Grades

Messenger
Motor Driver
Electric Truck Driver
Messroom Attendant
Caller-up
Engine Cleaner
Sand Drier
Shed Labourer

Stores Issuer
Telephone Attendant
Tube Cleaner
Axlebox Cleaner
Carriage Lampman
Globe Cleaner
Oiler

Shop, Etc., Staff

Acetylene Cutter
Bench Hand
Boiler Clothier
Brass Polisher
Brass Finisher's Mate
Canteen Assistant
Carriage Fitter
Checker
Cleaner – Frame or Wheel
Coil Winder
Core Maker
Drop Stamper
Electrician's Assistant
Electric Welder
Electric Plater
Electric Lamp Attendant
File Cutter
Fitter's Mate
Gas Meter Inspector
Grinder
Hammer Driver
Machinist – Wood
Messroom Attendant

Metal Dresser
Motor Truck Driver
Oxy-Actylene Burner
Painter
Painter, Coaching
Painter helper
PRO MAN
Rivetter
Screw Sorter
Scrap Sorter
Stay Tapper
Sewing Machinist
Store Keeper
Stores Issuer
Metal Worker
……………..
Trimmer's Mate

Miscellaneous Grades

Lift Attendant
Messenger

Telephone Attendant

Whilst most women left the workshops at the end of the war in accordance with Government and union agreements, a number were recruited yet again as hammer-drivers in the later 1940s to make up for the lack of manpower, lasting into the early 1950s. These recruits came through family contacts.

The women in the Trimming shop stayed but would have lost their jobs in the redundancies in the Carriage & Wagon Works amalgamation and final closure in 1967, ending women's presence in the factory.

NICKNAMES

The Legend

Do you have a 'nickname'? The Works was full of men with nicknames. Indeed, many were only known by their nickname. Some
names were purely descriptive – Lanky, others because of family
connections, like Big Arthur (the dad) Arthur (the son) and Little
Arth (the younger brother) – this despite the fact that none of their
names were Arthur! Others came with a 'back-story'.

Stephen Macmillan:

Black and Decker' ... why? One of the guys had a dodgy
heart, thus prone to fainting, hence, 'Black and Decker ... the
collapsible work-mate!

The Works' sense-of-humour is a notorious legend in its own right
from its earliest times. So here are some fondly remembered and
hilarious ones.

Alfred Williams:

Tubby – about the size of a thirty-six barrel; Baltimore – who
dressed in a scarlet tunic much too big; Jimmy Useless – a skilled
workman when the spirit moved him; Budget, Strawberry and
The Jersey Lily – an ex-seaman.

Ryan Conduit:

Biffo the Bear, Freddie Gloom, KO Kelly, Smokey Bowden,
Bunny Bill, Sailor Moon, The 'Reverend' Ken Claridge, Stumpy
Perret, Joe 90, Pete 'Benny' Goodman, Bojangles.

Dave Mulley:

9 Shop had The Concrete Gnome, Reggie The Gonk, The
Goat, Jock, Top Cat, Swish.

John J. Edmunds:

I was nicknamed Moley because (at the time) I looked like Adrian Mole from the TV programme. Another I remember was Stings. I don't remember his name other than Colin, all because he nearly cut off his finger on a mill and all he said was 'it stings!'

Jeremy Wilks:

We had a guy we called Caaaaa Paaaaak. He always told us how he parked his caaaaa in the caaaaa paaaak.

Philip Musty:

Don't forget Bonzo, Chirpy and Wacker Penney, and remember Charlie Woof Woof?

Ryan Conduit:

Chargehand in 19 shop coppersmiths – Goldie, who crashed a glider, but scratch built his own propane injection system for his car.

Gordon Dickinson:

My nickname was 'Leaner' … can't think why.

John J. Edmunds:

Chelvis, because he had a quiff like Elvis and a speech impediment (harsh I know but that's teenagers for you!).

Stephen Macmillan:

Ram-Rod, Smudger, Nobby, Bucket of Blood (sorry Ian), Headless Chicken (RIP), Nowhere Man, Babsey Boo, Eddie Shoestring, The Green Slug, Tom and Jerry, Geno, Midge, Golly, Block-Head, Luigi (Harry Roberts son???) PS … love the fact that Dave Mulley put in my old nickname Swish … why? I had so many earrings, looked like a swish curtain rail.

Andy Binks:

Bones, Kitchen, Blockhead, Swish, Dumpy, Stumpy, Long Pod, Green Slug, Bucket-of-Blood, Noddy, and Nobby, and, of course, Melvyn, otherwise known as Drill Head from when a drill fell on his head and floored him!

Strangely, the women didn't seem to go in for it!

Some 'nicknames' were passed from man to man as they 'came with the job'.

Machinery in the Works was originally, and for a long time, belt-driven. These would often become defective or simply break. Alfred Williams writes of the 'Strappie', as does Ken Gibbs decades later:

Ken Gibbs:

A broken belt from countershaft to machine could usually be put back by the chargehand, but a belt from the main-line shaft to the counter-shaft had to be replaced by the official 'Strappie'. This individual resided in a small screened off area in the O Shop, which was the Tool Room. His bench and screen walls were covered in pieces of belt of all sorts of sizes and materials from small round leather to 'VEE' belts and up to the heavy 10in to 12in width of belt used to drive the line shafting itself from its large wire-screened motor at the end of the line of roof columns.

Another who resided on a bench in the O Shop was 'the Clockie': There were so many clocks around the Works that one skilled man was employed to maintain and wind all the clocks once a week, which took him every day, Monday to Friday. He had a winding rota of which clocks had to be wound each day and as he went around he had a special watch, his mobile master clock, to which he re-set and adjusted the individual clocks. On two days of the year, when the clocks went forward and when the clocks went back, he was at his busiest!

INSIDERS' CODE

Many workplaces had or have a specific language or what is sometimes known as jargon. Knowing the 'language' or 'vocabulary' means you can work and operate in that environ. Sharing a 'code' with its own sub-text, history and understandings, however, means you are an 'Insider', a member of the gang. The Works had a lot of 'shared' vocabulary:

Coil a wire: turning the long, hot metal around and around – the operation necessary to 'make a spring'.

Crackers: (this one specific to painters) white spirit was always referred to as 'crackers'. If the paint was too thick you were told 'stir some crackers into it!'

Down the slope: being 'laid off' – it referred to the slope that led down to the tunnel under the railway and out to the 'outside'. In the winter it was always slippery and once you went down it, it was hard to get back up.

Doing time: a term that describes the time spent completing an apprenticeship.

Balance: the wage 'bonus' paid fortnightly in arrears.

Fluff house: the Asbestos House(s) for stripping out the asbestos.

Given up: when a lad had finished his apprenticeship he was 'given up', i.e. freed from the conditions of his Indentures.

Given-the-Bells: in the AE Shop fellow workers would strike the steel buffers of all the locomotives with their hammers so that they 'peeled-their-chimes' if someone tried to sneak in late – and also as a fond farewell for another poor blighter given the push and going out into the cold hard world!

Greenbacks: In the diesel era apprentices were known as 'Greenbacks' because of the green overalls they wore during their apprenticeship as opposed to the tradesman's blue. Boilermakers and welders for some reason had brown overalls with their number on the back.

I came out or **out of my time:** a phrase used in early times and still used by those trained in BR times to describe when they had finished their apprenticeship or training.

I got the DCM: I got the paper in my pay packet to tell me 'don't come Monday', i.e. my services were no longer required, most often apprentices who had just completed their time. In reality these words did not appear on the letter, but that is how they entered common usage.

Incomers: people who came from other places to live in Swindon.

Inside: what Swindoners called the Works. Those who worked inside Swindon Works were called 'insiders'. Local folklore, passed down through the generations, tells the story of the unfortunate young teacher, an 'incomer' to the town, i.e. not born and bred there. Trying to get to know his pupils better, he innocently asked one boy: 'Where does your father work?' 'Inside, Sir,' was the prompt reply. 'And mine, Sir.' 'Mine too Sir,' the chorus went up. The poor man was overwhelmed. How could so many children announce proudly that their fathers were detained working 'inside' His Majesty's prisons!

Knocking off time: in the early years, when most machines inside the Works were belt-driven, it was the custom at the end of the day to knock the belt off your machine, this gave rise to the saying!

Let go: not given a job on completion of apprenticeship, or being made redundant when work was slack.

New writes or **rewrites:** terms used by the sign-painters to describe their work. Novices would start on the 'rewrites' to learn the necessary techniques.

On the Club: off sick – stems from the time when each shop/shed would have its own Sick Fund Club that would pay them when they were off work from sickness or accident, but still in use by old railwaymen even today!

Shortening hands: laying off men.

Short time: not working the full hours or days in the week. This Damocles' Sword hung over generations of workmen in the Works right from its earliest times and particularly in the 'boom and bust' economic times of the nineteenth and early twentieth centuries.

Trip: this one word encapsulated the whole experience of the Works' annual holiday.

The Big E: in BR days this was a sick day with pay – you had to get your clock-card signed by a foreman. The men were entitled to three days a year sick pay without a doctor's certificate. These were referred to as E days, meaning 'entitled to pay'. Hence the derivative the BIG E.

The Grand March Past: on Pay Day the men would line up and 'march past' the Pay Tables put up in the shop.

Up the smoke: up to London.

Down the smoke: obviously down to Bristol.

Vagrancy List: vacancy list posted internally.

MOULDERS' CODE

'Shitters': Scrap castings

'Shank': ladle

'Fat': a fresh mix of sand

'Cope and drag': box parts (2)

'Rough Casting': as rough as a badger's ...!

'Short cast': not enough metal for mould

'A flyer, shut the window': a strained casting with excess metal around it; liable to 'fly'

'He's pregnant': a casting with a swelling

'Welsh riser': a mould that leaked metal while pouring

DID YOU KNOW?

Outsiders Work 'Inside'?

Evening Advertiser, Monday Sept 1960:

RAILMEN DEMAND ACTION
Swindon BR shopmen ask for pay rise. Nearly 1,000 Swindon railway shopmen called for an 8% minimum pay increase, back dated to Jan 4th and urged immediate steps to secure a £13 a week national minimum at a meeting held in Swindon Town Hall. They solidly rejected the offer of 3%.

Jim Masters, BR Loco Works AEU convenor, referred to the fact that under a guarantee arrangement men employed by outside firms at Swindon Works on the maintenance and repair of diesel units supplied by their firms to BR were doing the same sort of work as railwaymen alongside them, but the comparative rates were 'shocking'. The hourly rate paid by one firm was 8s 2d but the average total hourly rate for skilled craftsmen in the railway works was just over 6s.

The Foremen: 'Tin Gods in Bowler Hats!'

'See the foreman'... these words could chill the soul – mostly it meant you were in trouble. Not for nothing were the foremen known as 'Tin Gods'. On the shop floor the foremen wielded immense authority and power, even the Company realised this. Circulars addressed to foremen always spoke of 'your shop,' 'men under your control,' 'your men,' leaving little doubt as to who ran the show. The extent of their power is highlighted in the wording of the 1874 Rules:

> Infraction of the following Rules will be punished *at the discretion of the foreman*, [my italics] either by discharge, suspension or fine, the extent of the penalty being determined according to the nature of the offence, but no fine will in any case exceed 5/-.

This 'direct line of communication' between the Managers and the foremen became more formalised under G.J. Churchward, who set up 'working committees' involving his assistants, the foremen, their chargemen and the draughtsmen. It was a brilliant piece of 'man' and 'production' management. It was around this time, 1903, that the Foreman's Association was inaugurated to '*promote unity between members and the officers of the Company*'.

The foreman could make your life reasonable, even good, or the opposite – hell, especially if you got on his 'Black List'. He could help you make money, or not. He could put you on a good gang (i.e. a gang that worked well and made money) or a gang that never got the best jobs but got the worse ones. He could help you advance, or hold you back, especially when an apprentice. In early times he also held the ultimate power – he could 'hire *and* fire'.

John Attwell (1940s/50s):

The foremen were the people with influence – and we were at the mercy of which one we got. It was the foremen's prerogative to decide who was put in which gang, who was in charge of the gang, and which gang were given the best 'jobs' at the best prices.

There were times, however, when foremen played a decisive and defining role in the history of the Works and of the GWR, seeking the best for the workmen and their families. Perhaps the most iconic example was in 1847 when the GWR wanted to lay off hundreds of men but the foremen of the different shops held a meeting at which it was resolved to consent that the whole body should work short-time instead of so many hands being turned adrift at a time when they would have difficulty in procuring employment,

Foremen were also very able and clever men. They had to be. It was a job that came with demanding responsibilities. They managed incredible production projects, large budgets, numerous men, often in the hundreds, and all the other things that went into running a complex and, sometimes, specialised workshop.

A.E. 'Dusty' Durrant wrote:

The chief foreman, Mr Millard, presided over a gathering of under-foremen each with his group of charge-hands under whom came various tradesmen, apprentices and labourers. I do not know how many men were employed in A shop, doubtless well over a thousand, yet railway practice called the man in overall charge a mere foreman! In most places one-tenth of the size, outside the railway, he would be called at least works' manager, or even works' director.

The first foremen we know of come from Works' Manager Minard Rea's Memos, and John Fawcett's list:

Foreman and Contractors

On 1856 Notice sent by Minard Rea	As identified on John Fawcett's List 1865 written retrospectively
Mr Walter Mather	Second Foreman of Erecting Shop
Mr William Nicholson	First Foreman in Fitting & Turning Shop
Mr Thomas Stewart	Second Foreman in 'Smiths' Dept

Mr William Falconer	First Foreman of Wheel Turning Dept
Mr Richard Pattison	Third Foreman of Erecting Shop
Mr James Haydon	Third Foreman in Fitting & Turning Shop
Mr Thomas Rawlinson	First Foreman in Paint Shop
Mr Samuel Gray	First Foreman in Patternmakers Dept
Mr Robert Laxon	First Foreman in Coppersmith Dept
Mr Thomas Jones	First Foreman of Masons Dept

Swindon Loco Works' Foremen's first outing to Symonds Yat on Saturday 24 August 1895.
Back row I to r: D. Clark, J. Townsend, C. Tincknell, J. Thomas, A. Nash, R. Pattison, G. Dingley, W.S. Sheppard, D. White, C. Tigh, W. Morgan, R. Harris, W. Hunt, (hon. Sec.) S. Thrasher, F. Hopkins.
Middle row I to r: T. Veness, W. Chivers, H. Hayward, G. Willis, T. Watson, L. Dyer, J. Burrows, R. Baker, F. Apted, E. Noad, J. Hunt.
Front row I to r: F. Laxon, J. Faulkner, T. Patterson, J. Smith, A. Mizen (set back) G. Webb (Manager's Office), G. Townsend, B. Hale (set back) H. Barrett, G. Seath, T. Hardiman.

Count the bowlers. The bowler was the Foreman's symbol of status.
'Look out – the Bowler' was a warning cry men would pass to each other as the foreman approached!

What the workmen expected from a foreman was 'hard', what they hoped for was 'fair' – a few were both. Alfred Williams did not hold much truck with foremen, seeing in them all that he hated about the Works, but even he admitted that some were 'humane':

> Most foremen are excessively autocratic and severe with their men, denying them the slightest privilege or relaxation of the iron laws of the factory. Others are of a wheedling, pseudo-fatherly type, who, by a combination of professed paternal regard and a cunning manipulation of the reins, contrive to make everything they do appear just and reasonable and so hold their men in complete subjection. Some foremen, again, are of the ceremonious order, who, from pure vanity will insist upon the complete observance of the most trivial detail and drive their work-men half way to distraction. A few, on the other hand, are generous and humane. They hold the reins slack, and, without the knowledge of their chiefs, grant a few small privileges and are rewarded with the confidence of their work-men and a willingness to labour on their part amounting to enthusiasm.

Foremen generally came up through the ranks so they knew the work, they knew the nature of the men on the shop floor and they knew the tricks and cons that could be pulled. There were times, however, when it was not *what* you knew but *who* you knew that got you the foreman's job.

The tradition of sons following fathers into the Works meant a small number of families could boast a foreman down through the generations, some stepping into their forebears' shoes:

Circular No 28 January 1891
Mr F Laxon has been appointed to succeed his late father as foreman in the K Shop.

John Walters and Roger Hayes were both foremen in the latter days of the Works; both had 'foreman' in their blood. John's father, Jack, was a boilermaker, who became foreman and later head foreman; both Roger's grandfathers were foremen before him. Grandfather Hayes was foreman of the Locomotive trial gang, which tested locomotives following general repairs in the workshop, and grandfather Godsell was foreman in C & W workshops. Both men went on to become head foremen at the same time and appear in the official photograph of 'Officers and Foreman' 1931 taken outside the Main Offices. These official photographs were taken every ten years and make fascinating perusal capturing as they do some of the great names in the 'management' history of the Works. John Walters was the last President of the Foreman's Association, which changed to a purely social function *c*. 1950 and finally ended in 1993.

After the Second World War there was a marked change in people's attitudes and expectations, especially amongst the men returning from the experiences of war. There was a small shift in power structures that crept into the Works, yet, even a long time after Nationalisation of the railways, well into the 'liberated '60s', the foreman's word held sway, as many young new journeymen found.

With the rise of the unions the foreman's powers lessened. Now it was a time of 'negotiation' and more subtle 'management'. Even so, one had to tread carefully. Works' folklore tells of a 'band of brothers' in the 1970s, the foremen of 15 Shop, a formidable group of men who looked out for each other, so much so, it is whispered, that they were generally called 'the Mafia'.

It is said the foreman's maxim was:

If it is difficult we'll do it immediately. If it is impossible, it may take a little longer!

Undoubtedly 'the foreman', working with both the men and 'the officials', played a significant role in shaping the history of the Works, the GWR, and of Swindon town – something to be remembered.

P AND R

Prosthesis

The Works (and the railways) had a bad reputation for workmen losing their lives, but many more lost their limbs. So many men lost limbs working on the GWR system that the Company offered 'artificial limbs' with 'work carried out between three departments which have to do with the substances involved, wood, leather and metal'. The first artificial limb made was in 1878, which was for an unfortunate man named Harris who, having been run over by a train, had to have his legs amputated. Luckily he was a Medical Fund Society member. Even with this the legendary Works' pride in the job was present as, not content to offer just 'a peg-leg' replacement, by using the technical expertise of the engineer and the skill of the carpenter craftsman, they created a wooden limb with 'sockets' that offered more flexibility.

By the 1880s this work came under the jurisdiction of the Engineering Committee, as Extracts from the Minutes of the Meeting, which reported on workmen who required such limbs, shows:

January 1889 – John Ellis, Engineman of Dredger at Great Western Docks, Rymouth

'met with an accident resulting in amputation of both legs. Authority was given to supply Ellis with two artificial legs from Swindon.'

April 1889 – Arthur Cooke, labourer at Worcester

'left arm was amputated consequent upon an accident. Authority was given to supply an artificial arm from Swindon.'

February 1895 – David Davies, ganger at Shrewsbury

'accident resulting in the loss of his right leg. It was agreed to provide him with an artificial leg to be made at Swindon.'

February 1896 – Edwin Mitchel, labourer Telegraph Department
'resulting in the loss of his right leg. Authority was given.'

January 1897 – Henry Plant, packer, and John Whitcombe, ballast guard
Both lost a foot and in each case authority was given to be supplied with an artificial one made at Swindon.

The 'limbs' could also be returned for repair and/or alteration.

The men who worked on the artificial limbs, fitters, trimmers, carpenters and polishers, were highly skilled and their work was costed into the production. A small record book entitled 'Art. Limbs No3 1893–1896' gives details of 'New Work' and 'Repairs' for legs and arms and crutches:

New Work:

Green Amer: Morocco	sq ft 1½
Horse hair (old)	lb. ¼
Calico	yd. ⅛ × 60
Polish	pint ¼
Leather trimmers	1/10d
Polishers	3d/
Estimated to cost about	13/-

Repairs:

J Walters Swindon Station
Repairs to Artificial Leg.

Brace webbing	2 " yards 1 ¼
Elastic webbing	" ⅓
Glass string leather	lb. ½
3 hrs E Clarke Leather trimmers	1/7d

Special consideration was given to the interests of the individuals so that sports people had legs of beech wood rather than the customary willow and others were given hands that had adaptations for holding pens so they could write. A GWR *Magazine* article (1940) tells of the

intricacies involved in producing: 'a model of a human hand fashioned from willow … with a combination of little devices, knuckle joints and hidden springs that allow the thumb and finger to execute normal movements.' By the 1930s some 4,000 limbs had been issued and one of these was given to the renowned Works photographer William Hooper, who lost his leg as a result of an accident with the impressive traverser in B Shed in 1886. After the First World War the company offered prostheses free-of-charge to returning men who had lost limbs in 'the service of their Country'.

Artificial limbs made in the Works were still being maintained in 1960 and a few were made as replacements, but with the retiring of the Chargeman specialist doing the work at this time such work ceased.

Rehabilitation

After the Second World War there was a realisation of the need for rehabilitation to get workers back to work as quickly as possible to enable the country's economic recovery. Vauxhall Motors Rehabilitation Unit became the role model for others to follow, including the nationalised railway. In 1951 a plan was evolved to set up a unit for those in the railway industry and in mid-1953 a 'rehabilitation' workshop was introduced (although not formally 'opened' until May 1954) on the edge of the Works in C & W 7 Shop, located in London Street, for 'patients' (their term) in 'the Swindon District'. It was 'well equipped, air-conditioned with a capacity for about 35 patients.'

Working to the definition as stated in their 1954 publicity pamphlet:

Rehabilitation is the active process that leads to the restoration of the handicapped
to the fullest physical, mental, social, vocational and economic usefulness
for which they are capable in the shortest possible time

and with the ethos of 'PRODUCTIVE WORK', it assisted local railway workmen recovering from injury and, perhaps surprisingly, from various kinds of operations not apparently work related. They worked on specially modified machines that produced components for actual use in the factory. Admission to the programme was voluntary and was 'time limited', most attended for a day or two, while, a record of attendees shows, the longest periods appear to be three to four weeks.

The *British Transport Commission – Western Region Record Sheet Of Employee Receiving Treatment In Rehabilitation Workshop (15b Shop)* shows that even injuries incurred outside working hours could also be treated within the unit. That of Henry Garbutt records:

Nature of Disability: Injured right wrist – fell from bicycle, off duty, 18.1.58.
Date Entered Workshop: 29.1.58
Date Left Workshop: 7.2.58

Other 'outside' injuries treated include ones from 'motorbike accident' and 'playing football'. The nature of the work-related injuries were fractures of all limbs and fingers and thumbs, ankles and feet, bad bruising from falls or things falling on them, neck and back problems, and eyes. The 1954 pamphlet claims, 'Nearly 95 per cent of the cases that have passed though the workshop have returned to their normal work.'

It did not matter the nature of the patient's occupation as they exercised on machines and equipment suited to their disability. These machines (simple presses, punches and drills) could be adapted and modified to deliver the required physical movement for repetitive actions.

The Rehabilitation Centre was itself a casualty, it was also closed when the C & W Department was finally closed in 1967.

The Tunnel

At one time there were around thirteen entrances into the Works but only one carried particular significance, the 1870 Main Entrance that leads to a long subway that runs northwards beneath the mainline railway tracks. This is known to all in Swindon, especially those who worked 'Inside', as 'the tunnel':

> The new tunnel entrance to the GWR's Company's Works at New Swindon is so far advanced towards completion that it was used for the first time Saturday last. The entrance to the tunnel will be immediately in front of the Mechanic's Institution and the exit in front of the Timekeeper's offices on the other side of the line, a distance of about 100 yards.
>
> *Wiltshire Independent*, Thursday 10 February 1870

The tunnel is built under the route of the original 'Workmens' East Gate Entrance', which took them across the mainline tracks to get to work each morning and return home each night – a dangerous enterprise. The stone entrance, an imposing archway under a wide gable, with a smaller one on each side, is within the length of the

Works' 'boundary' wall that was part of the original Carriage Works. It is part of Emlyn Square, centred between the original central avenues of the Square. It was located here so that workers could easily enter and leave the Works via the village, where many of them would have been living at that time. It is some 389ft (115.8m) long, 15ft (4.6m) wide and 7ft (2.1m) high. Going down the tunnel could seem a long way, especially if you were late:

Maurice Wilby:

I dragged myself through it in the mornings – and ran out of it at five to the Glue Pot.

The tunnel was rather atmospheric as in all its working life it would have been rather dark, being but dimly lit and somewhat damp and dank so that often the ground was slippery underfoot. At the end (near the Main Office block) was a slope that was going 'up' going in, but going 'down' going out. In wet or damp conditions this slope was rather slippery. It gave rise to the 'Insider's' too often used phrase – 'going down the slippery slope' – used if someone had lost their job or not been kept on at the end of their apprenticeship. Its roof of brick jack-arches springing from cast-iron beams and brick walls and ground created an echoing quality and, as Ian Williams remembers, 'some men would sing or whistle when passing through the tunnel, it had an acoustic character to the sound and was quite pleasant at times.' Added to that the rumble of the trains running immediately overhead would enhance the feeling of being 'underground' and even 'dungeon-like', as some describe it.

When the workers were 'Inside' the doors of the entrances remained firmly closed. In the 1870s, an 'iron turnstile at the entrance controlled the flow of traffic in and out of the Works. Many of those who worked 'Inside' will remember, as a young lad, being sent a letter asking them to 'report to the Main Entrance' on their first morning, and they would do so, just inside the tunnel at the 'Enquiry/Watchman's Office'. On the facing side was the GWR Savings Bank office, which later became the 'Priv' Ticket office where the Works' employees could collect their 'special' rates train tickets.

The watchman on duty would be checking not just *who* went in *and* came out, but, just as importantly, *what* went in – as the tunnel was also used for deliveries that had to be regulated so as not to clash with the workers' going-in and coming-out times:

Nora Hunt (1927):

The Main Offices were reached via the tunnel entrance – a long paved tunnel running under the mass of main lines, with only lamp lighting. Along this echoing tunnel came two shire horses hauling their heavy load of what appeared to be locked black coffins on a flat-bed wagon [delivery of the wages money to the factory from the bank] their clattering hoofs echoing with the overhead train rumbles. They were trained to perform this task to perfection, as the tunnel ended in a steep left-hand slope to again reach ground level, so about half way through they would develop a steady trot, then gather speed as they hauled their burden up the slope – no mean feat on a slippery morning.

Even more important was what came *out*. In the later years 'the Watchman' became 'Security', sometimes with an Alsatian dog, such was the outward flow of contraband.

Ian Williams:

When walking out you'd hear guys saying 'security on the gate' and then some of those who had purloined something would panic, often leaving the bits and pieces at the side of the tunnel somewhere along its length. You would see pots of paint and bits of wood etc., lying there.

There were more elaborate stories of what went on through and out of the tunnel, such as the man who had a 'chitty' for a barrow load of firewood that he took home each day, until they found out all the wheelbarrows were going missing.

Above 'the tunnel' entrance one could read the changing course of history of the Works passing through the different 'ownerships' and amalgamations, as the names, boards and signs changed. Today 'the tunnel' is one of Swindon's most famous and much loved landmarks, a physical connection to the past – still touched with memories:

The Tunnel

The tunnel lies cold and still in the night
Save for the sound of water from dripping walls
Everything's sleeping the long hours through
'Til the hustle and bustle of daybreak calls.

Come ten-to-nine and from every direction
Men and women of mixed collections
Surge into the coldness and stillness there
'Til talk and clatter fill the air.

Some hurry, some dawdle and others run
Each to his work, a new day begun
Some smile and make merry, while others are sad
But they all follow where others have trod.

The light at the mouth is cold and grey
Then it blushes gold in the heat of the day
Softens and reddens as night draws nigh
And the stars appear with the Hooter's cry.

Have past five that glorious hour
The faces lift within the tower
Of offices, as work comes to an end
Then down the slope the mob descends.

The tunnel fills with noise once more
Each one his aim to reach the door
To freedom, until another dawn
And work once more with stifled yawn.

Lorna Dawes, Clerk.

The last tramp of workmen's feet through the tunnel was a sad affair at the closing of the Works.

Today the tunnel has been upgraded and is a conduit between Swindon's town centre and the regenerated Works' site. It is part of the Grade II Listed Buildings.

DID YOU KNOW?

Dinosaurs?

In 1950 an unexpected excitement came to the Works in a form that no one could ever have foreseen. Dinosaurs!

PREHISTORIC BONES AT SWINDON
Fossilised bones recently unearthed during excavations for the new British Railways Western Region's buildings at Swindon have been submitted to the natural history section of the British Museum and identified as vertebral bones from the neck of an ichthyosaurus, a fossil swimming reptile.
Gloucestershire Echo, Tuesday 26 September 1950

Two vertebral bones of this ichthyosaurus were presented by K.J. Cook, M & E Engineer, Loco Works, to Swindon Council and thence the museum.

Just twenty-five years later, in May 1975, yet another discovery, even more exciting! Excavations in the non-ferrous foundry for the foundation of a sand reclamation plant created the opportunity for a fascinating find. Seven feet down, 18in deeper than previous foundations, workmen found part of a skull. Its significance was not immediately recognised but discussions by 'learned people' at the British Museum and the University of Wales decided it was part of the skeleton of a prehistoric monster! It was requested that as much as possible it should be carefully retrieved, so while production in the foundry continued, the bones were gradually accumulated.

As they discovered more it was not sure if there were one or even two fossilised creatures. The fossilised remains appeared to be of a fish-like reptile but even the 'experts' were puzzled. First it was thought to be an ichthyosaurus, then a opthalmosaurus but mixed up with plesiosaurus, then finally, it was agreed by Professors Appleby and Halstead of Cardiff and Reading Universities respectively, that it definitely was an opthalmosaurus *and* a pliosaurus brachyspondylus, a rare air-breathing creature that had lived and apparently been about Swindon some 130–150 million years ago and to top it all – the most complete example of its kind ever found.

Huge excitement followed and requests from television programmers came to be allowed to 'show it off'! Works' Manager Harry Roberts decided Blue Peter should have the honour. For the television presentation the bones were laid out on an expanded polystyrene shape to give the viewers an idea of what the beast would have looked like when alive. The photo shows the 'Plio' on its 'bed' outside the Main Offices. On Thursday 22 May 1975 it went 'on air'. When the bones were returned they were exhibited at Swindon Museum, arousing great interest as some 5,000 people came to 'meet' this new celebrity. Now it resides somewhere in the Natural History Museum.

4
THE NOT-SO-GOOD BITS

Conditions

The Works, by its very nature, was an extremely dirty, noisy, smelly, unhealthy place in the time of steam, and only comparatively less so in the age of diesel. The conditions and noise changed little over the decades until the stricter standards of Health and Safety and requirements under various Factory Acts.

Alfred Williams – Hammerman 1915 described it as 'positively tortuous':

> the dense smoke and fumes from the oil forges, and the thick sharp dust and ashes from the coke fires ... a great number of accidents are due directly or indirectly to the unhealthy air about the place ... the heat is far more painful to endure ... especially in close and stuffy shed ... it will be impossible for the work men to maintain any degree of strength or vigour ... the temperature in front of the furnaces will be considerably over 100 degrees and when the air is stagnant and thick and heavy with nauseous smoke and fumes ... it is positively tortuous ... the perspiration seems to be drawn from your bones ... .

Mrs Phyllis Saunders – Blacksmith's F1 Shop (Second World War) had much the same experience during her time:

> It was a terrible place to have to work. It was filthy. There was not much air. There was a few windows at the top, almost up

at the roof. They were seldom opened because they were a job to get to, but we did open them at times because the walls and everything got so filthy. We had great big fires where I was. We had great big hoses there too, 'cos every night when you've finished work one of the men would hose down the dirt floor to settle the dust … all where you worked, and dampened it down 'cos dust used to fly up if it got hot and dry and made it terrible. It got so hot with all those open fires. I picked up a bad throat, just off diphtheria. I think it was all the dirt probably. I had some time off and the doctor treated it with Penicillin – that was twice!

Many war-recruited women struggled. **Mrs Enid Saunders – The Tube Shop (Second World War):**

I had to work in the Tube House. It was a most horrible place. It was really dirty and you never felt clean. … It was only a small place made in corrugated iron, an extension of the L2 Shop. In the night we could hear something creepy, crawly and it was rats running up and down the tubes. Those rats were very frightening. They would scrabble all up the tubes. Oh it was a *horrible* place!

It was no better in some of the shops in the C & W department. **Jim Rogers:**

On 1 November 1939 I went 'Inside'. My first job was in the C & W Stamping House, 18 Shop. Dreadful it was. The first impression was that it was very dirty, very noisy and very dark. The lighting was gas lighting, not very bright and it seemed all you could see was the fire of the furnaces.

The era of the diesel held promise for change, a better, cleaner environment. It was a change in that it was different, but some found it just as bad, and in some respects worse. The oil got into everything.

The poor conditions extended to those facilities of a more private nature – the toilets. The standard of toilet provision for the men was primitive in the extreme. Lack of privacy (a large hole in the door ensured one could always be on view), lack of dignity from the necessity of 'sharing' of a plank seat and flowing water down the trough, and lack of time 'to-go' as the toilet attendant kept tabs on the permitted timescale, made things worse. This state of affairs changed little over the decades.

Dusty Durrant – apprentice in the 1940s:

In the yard between R and G Shops, dating from the original works, was a very primitive form of lavatory having a row of cubicles whose seat was placed over an open drain through which water flowed continuously.

Even as late as the swinging sixties nothing much had changed, causing headlines in the local paper:

CONDITIONS IN BR WORKS ARE CRITICISED
Condition in Swindon railway works came in for strong criticism from a trade unionist on Wednesday. An Amalgamated Engineering Union representative, Mr J Chequer, at Swindon Trades Council told members: 'I am no British Rail employee, but last week I visited the Works, the antiquated washing facilities and toilets appalled me. If the British Transport Commission were private individuals they would be jailed'.

Wiltshire Gazette & Herald, 1966

This public criticism must have done the trick because these toilets were refurbished and updated at great cost, only to be demolished a few years later!

DID YOU KNOW?

Smells

Roy Taylor:

It was queer because when I started in 1938 I was told to come in clean clothes and then I got put into the scraggery where it was filthy! My overwhelming memory of in there was it smelt like anything. It was that 'white water' they used to work the machines, a mixture of water and rape oil.

John Charlesworth:

It had a smell of its own that scraggery with the white water you know. You could smell it a mile away.

Ken Gibbs:

There was the distinctive, and to any steam enthusiast, marvellous smell – the aroma of oily steam and warm lubricating oil which can only emanate from a steam engine – the smell of the steam engine.

Jack Hayward:

At the west corner of the foundry was the cupola where the cast iron was produced. ... The pour had to be made before the temperature of the molten iron dropped to a certain level. ... As the pour was being made so the boxes released a cloud of grey smoke accompanied by a most obnoxious acrid stench that not only filled the foundry but also permeated the air up to half a mile away. ... After the casting had been allowed to set the pegs holding the boxes together would be knocked out and the casting separated from the dry sand polluting the air with evil smelling dust.

John Mudge:

Dirt can be brushed off, but the oil drips!!! They would start off as a 5p then spread out into a 10p, then merge with other drips and become bigger still. Your overalls could stand up on their own. Horrible it was. My mum would say, 'What's that funny smell?' It was the oil. It used to get in your hair too. You couldn't get rid of that smell. Even later when we worked on the Maybachs there was that smell.

Robert Chester:

The all-pervading smell of engineering excellence in progress, It was ever present, everywhere. The smell was generated by the use of heat through forges, cutting torches, welding gear, machine shop smells of hot swarf, cutting oils and lubricants (wasn't it 10 per cent oil and 90 per cent water lads?) , diesel, hydraulic oil etc., etc.

Malcolm Holland:

As for the all-pervading smell of engineering, I recall 19 Shop seemed to always smell of disinfectant, mind you what the underside of those DMU's were coated in, it was hardly surprising, no toilet holding tanks in those days!

Stan Scott:

The entire Works had an assortment of smells but for me the most memorable was the smell of steam heating pipes throughout the Works. These hot metal pipes leaking steam were under-floor beneath metal grills and also on the walls around the workshop, usually too high to offer much warmth.

Dimity Linsell:

I remember shop keepers in town knowing people from the Works by the smell when they went into the shops.

Fatal Accidents

Swindon Works, by its very nature, was a dangerous place, at any time, from its beginning to its end. During the nineteenth century the Works had something of a bad reputation because of the number and frequency of *fatal* accidents. The causes of the accidents could be put down to a number of things – workers' carelessness, difficult and horrendous conditions, over-work, inexperience, lack of supervision, inattention, youth, old age, bad luck. The Company instigated a number of Rules to try to ensure a safer environment. Rule 24 of the Book of Rules and Regulations states, '*Servants of the Company must not expose themselves to danger.*' Unhappily for the Company the press were happy to bring these fatalities to the attention of their readers and take the Company to task.

In September 1866 *The Swindon Advertiser and North Wilts Chronicle* remarked:

> In the 1850s there was some comment on the large number of accidents that happened, some were obviously due to the carelessness of the workmen, but more to bad working conditions.

In October it reported on the 'important revelations of over-work [by the] railway employees here' stating: 'I suppose there will be no improvement in the condition of the men until some terrible accident is clearly traced to this overwork.'

DREADFUL ACCIDENT AT THE NEW SWINDON FACTORY

On Wednesday morning, as Henry Golding, a man employed to oil and clean the machinery in the boiler shop was in the act of cleaning one of the punching machines, the strap with which the machine is driven got connected with the driving shaft and the machine started working. The consequence was that the poor fellow's right arm got drawn in between the two cog wheels, completely smashing the arm as it went, this drew his body against a projecting piece of the machine which entered his right side, which was completely forced in. He was taken to the Union Railway house where he now lies (Wednesday) but it is impossible he can live out the night.

Reading Mercury, Saturday 22 March 1851

Dreadful accidents were not confined to the 1850s, as subsequent articles in the press and reports to the GWR Board show. The numerous accidents of the following decades also make horrific reading. Lads, no matter their background, seemed particularly susceptible to injury and death:

FATAL ACCIDENT IN SWINDON RAILWAY WORKS

On Wednesday last an accident that proved fatal, happened to one of the pupils, the eldest son of J Stoddart, Esq., formerly superintendent at Swindon Station. Evidently thinking there would be time to pass across the line between trucks before one that was in motion could reach some others that were to the left of him, he attempted to cross the rails and before he could do so was caught by the buffer of the approaching truck and forced with fearful violence against the buffer of another truck. Assistance was immediately at hand and the deceased was at once carried to his lodgings where he was attended by Dr Swinhoe. The internal injuries he had received, however, were beyond medical aid and he expired on Friday morning.

Reading Mercury, Saturday 21 July 1860

In 1862 William Morris wrote:

The fearful death of a lad named Leech occurred in the Swindon Railway Works, in consequence of his entanglement in the driving straps connecting some powerful machinery. This lad, although but twelve years of age, had for some time been engaged in the good work of earning his own livelihood by honest labour. He was a good lad and a great favourite with the men in the shop in which he worked.

Many more lads were to follow:

DISTRESSING ACCIDENT

A serious accident befell a boy named Hall, 14 years of age, living with his parents in Rodborne-lane, in the GWR factory yesterday afternoon. Hall, who had only been at work a day or two, was employed shunting some empty horse-boxes, and when turning round to disengage the horse from the couplings, got his foot stuck in the points. Before he could extricate it he was run over by the vehicle he was moving, his thigh, side and arm being so severely crushed, that little hopes are entertained for his recovery. He was taken to the Medical Society's hospital where the leg was amputated.

Gloucester Citizen, Friday 14 February 1890

ACCIDENT IN THE WORKS

An accident occurred on Monday in the R (turners) shop of the GWR Works, to a boy named Richard Rice. The lad was at work at a grinding or polishing machine and his coat became entangled in the machinery. Rice was drawn in and his right side and shoulder were injured besides severe injury being caused to his back. He was removed to the GWR's Medical Society's Accident Hospital.

Gloucester Citizen, Tuesday 20 May 1890

FATAL ACCIDENT

A terrible accident occurred in the 'D' shop of the GWR Works on Monday afternoon. A lad named Pinnegar, aged about fourteen, was engaged upon a machine for the cutting of tyres for the wheels of railway carriages. Pinnegar, who was rather short-sighted, was looking down to see if his work was placed in the right position, when going too near the large wheel, he was knocked down between the chisel and another part of the machine. The top of the poor boy's head was cut off completely. Death, of course, was instantaneous. Deceased's father, about six years ago, was killed on the railway, while returning home from work.

Western Gazette, Friday 18 September 1891

… and just a few days later:

ACCIDENT AT THE WORKS

A painful accident occurred in the GWR Works on Saturday morning. A lad named Pearce was working a lathe, and attempted, contrary to regulations, to clean his machine whilst in motion with the result that his thumb was literally torn out, sinews and all. He was detained at the Accident Hospital.

Gloucester Citizen, Monday 28 September 1891

It seems incredible that anyone would attempt to do this with their machine in motion, but obviously lots did because the GWR issued many notices, rules and directives to try to prevent it:

Rule Book No 33

The moving parts of any Engine, Crane, Lathe or other machine must not be oiled or cleaned while in motion. … The parts of the lathe or machine must not be changed while in motion.

No workman must attempt to put on a strap or interfere with the main shafting in anyway while the engine is in motion.

It is most important that workmen employed on lathes and other machines, should wear close fitting jackets.

Circular No 3369

Factory Acts Regulations for the guidance of Workmen – Clothing
Several cases have recently occurred where accidents have been due to clothing being caught in machinery. This principally applies to jackets with loose sleeves being worn and I shall be glad if you will take immediate steps to ensure that the following regulations are complied with: Clothing – No-one be allowed to work any kind of machine in loosely fitting clothes.

A spate of accidents in the early 1870s caused more comment in the local papers, much to the embarrassment of the Company, which issued this circular to try to stem the tide of criticism:

Circular

Nov 14th 1874

To All Foremen

Several cases have recently occurred in the Factory without the accident being reported to this office. The Company has been censured in the Daily Paper for their neglect in this matter. I must beg to call the particular attention of all Foremen to the importance of reporting all accidents in which the person injured is unable to return to his work by nine o'clock the following day. I trust this matter will be strictly carried out in the future.

Yours truly S Carlton, per J Haydon

Yet accidents remained commonplace throughout the Works' history and two of the more common reasons were being 'knocked down' and/or being 'run over':

SHOCKING RAILWAY ACCIDENT

A dreadful accident occurred in the GWR Works at New Swindon on Tuesday, a young man named William Butler of Wroughton, being run over by some freight trucks. His injuries were so serious that it was found necessary to amputate both legs. The operation was performed in the Accident Hospital where the poor fellow died on Tuesday night.

Gloucester Citizen, Thursday 23 November 1893

REPORT TO THE BOARD

Fatal accident to Blacksmith William Clarke

At Swindon 30th October 1894.

On the morning of 30th Oct., last Clarke was crossing the line on his way to the Engine Shed to work, when he was knocked down by an engine and killed.

Clarke was 75½ years of age and had been in the service of the Company 40⁷/₁₂ years, his rate of wages was 6/- per day. He has left a widow in very poor circumstances. She is practically dependent upon a married daughter for support.

THE NOT-SO-GOOD BITS

FATALITY IN THE SWINDON WORKS

It has been reported to the North Wilts Coroner that a fatality occurred on Friday in the GWR factory at Swindon. A workman, William Ealey … was passing from one part of the Works to another when he was knocked down by a shunting engine. He was at once removed to the Accident Hospital but his injuries were so terrible that the case was hopeless, death supervening within an hour of admission to the hospital.

Gloucester Citizen, 5 February 1910

Again the GWR did its bit to try minimise such accidents. One can read its absolute frustration in this memo even to threatening the ultimate punishment – instant dismissal:

Memo
28 Nov 1910
It is noticed that messenger boys are frequently passing over the crossing in front of these Offices instead of making use of the subway, and that last week four lads narrowly escaped being knocked down by an engine on the fast road.

I shall be glad if you will give very definite instructions to all concerned that the subway must be used for crossing the railway and that everyone disregarding this instruction will render himself liable to instant dismissal.
Sgd Churchward

Being in the wrong place at the wrong time, a lapse of concentration, or perhaps a lack of experience led to others:

REPORT TO THE BOARD
Fatal Accident to Labourer Thomas R S Messenger
At Swindon 14th Dec 1894

On 4th Dec last as Messenger was assisting to stack elm planks in the Timber Yard, he placed the 'stick' in the wrong position with the result that when the plank was moved the stick flew up and struck him in the head fracturing his skull. He died on the 16th Dec.

Messenger was 32 years of age and had been in the service of the Company 5⁵/₁₂ years, his rate of wages was 3/2 per day. He leaves a widow and three young children in destitute circumstances, the last child was born on the morning of the accident.

FATALITY AT SWINDON RAILWAY WORKS
KILLED BY A CRANE

On Saturday a shocking accident occurred in the Works resulting in fatal injuries to a man named Albert Hobbs, aged 30 who was employed in the factory in the capacity of a labourer. ... It would appear that Hobbs was standing near a crane which was in motion when it swung round and struck him violently, inflicting very serious injuries. The unfortunate man was removed most promptly to the Great Western Railway Medical Fund Society's Hospital, but it was at once apparent to everyone that his injuries were of such a terrible character as to place him beyond the aid of surgical skill. Everything that was possible was done for the sufferer, who, however, succumbed to internal injuries. The deceased leaves a widow and three children.

Gloucester Journal, Saturday 28 December 1901

Even into the twentieth century such accidents continued to occur. Alfred Williams wrote bitterly about this loss of life, seeing it in brutal terms. Writing of the 'night shift' he tells of the fatal injury to 'Smamer's brother' who was:

killed at the drop-stamps with a blow on the head ... A jagged piece of steel, ten or twelve pounds in weight, flew from the die and struck him between the eye and ear knocking out half his brains. As things go, no-one was to blame ... but he was murdered, all the same – done to death by the system that is responsible for the rash haste and frenzy such as is common on the night shift.

THE NOT-SO-GOOD BITS

FATAL ACCIDENT AT SWINDON
MACHINE WORKER KILLED IN G.W.R. WORKS

A fatal accident occurred in the Swindon GWR Works when Gordon Richard Kendrick ... was crushed to death.

It is stated that Kendrick, who was employed in the shop where the permanent way fittings are made, was by some means dragged into the machine he was working on and so badly was his body crushed that he died before Dr P.J. Filose arrived at the Works.

Western Daily Press, Thursday 7 September 1933

The accidents continued into British Railway times, although as Health and Safety progressed and stricter measures were enforced, fatalities occurred less often.

British Railways (Western Region)   B.R. 14433

....

ACCIDENT STATEMENT FORM

Date of Accident: *10th February 1961*   Name of Injured Person: *Davis Samuel*

Locality: *Bay 6, V Shop, Loco works.*   Grade: *Crane driver V/7264*

Station paid at: *Swindon*   Shop: *V*

GOOD TURN LED TO DEATH OF CRANE DRIVER

A good turn for a friend in need cost a crane-driver, Mr Samuel Davis (65) his life a week before his retirement, after more than 40 years' service, a Swindon Inquest was told. He was crushed to death between the arm of a crane and a pillar last Friday. He was returning to his own crane after seeing to a fault on the one driven by his mate.

Evening Advertiser, 15 February 1961

The last known fatal accident occurred when Cliff Slade was leaving the Works Committee Office and fell down the flight of wooden stairs and died.

Industrial Injuries

There were many ways to be permanently bodily damaged in the Works, either through accidents or industrial-induced effects.

Industrial Deafness

For some trades in the Works this was an expected outcome. Noise-induced hearing loss, tinnitus (a constant ringing in the ear) or total deafness just went with the job as incredible noise was an ever-present factor in the working day and night. Boilermakers and riveters often relied on lip-reading at work because the noise levels prevented any verbal communication. Hammermen and others working machinery also had unremitting noise levels to deal with.

In 1891 A.H. Malan, railway enthusiast, wrote a piece entitled 'A Look Round Swindon Works' in *The English Illustrated Magazine* making just this point:

Noise, indeed, there is more or less everywhere throughout this busy hive, but the finest effects of genuine ear-splitting clatter are naturally met with in the riveting shops. Hydraulic riveters … do all the work within their reach, just giving one noiseless 'squelch' with their great crab-like callipers upon the red-hot iron … But where those silent workers cannot operate, for lack of space or other reason, there *human* riveters are in all their glory, showing their appreciation of the pandemonium they create, by performing merry ratatans with their hammers at every moment of waiting. It is sad to think that these men seem all doomed to be deaf, but on the whole this appears to be a merciful dispensation than if they were doomed to retain the faculty of hearing unimpaired.

Writing nearly a quarter of a century later in 1914, Works' 'hammer-man' Alfred Williams describes the noise too:

The tremendous noise of the hammers and machinery and the priming of the boilers have a most injurious effect upon the body as well as the nervous system, it is all intensely painful and wearisome to the workmen... .

Decades later, in the 1950s, a new clerical recruit for the Blacksmith's shop office, Jack Hayward, remembers:

> We continued on our way down the shop, through this industrial fog accompanied by the din of steam hammers pounding on hot metal, and the high pitched scream of this huge saw cutting through hot metal as easy as a hot knife cuts through butter.

Long after Nationalisation 'noise pollution' was still a problem and in the 1970s, when people were more aware of their 'rights', Brian Maddicks claimed and received £2,000 compensation for hearing loss from the effects of being constantly beside the engine 'test beds' waiting for engines to come off on to the trailers, on which he worked.

In the 2000s many ex-railwaymen claimed and won compensation for their hearing problems. One, reported in the local press, worked as a fitter between 1962 and 1986. He claimed he was not given ear protection or advice:

> When I started it was the modern age of the railway that was starting. We had modern workshops, modern ways of teaching, but we weren't taught about Health and Safety in that respect. If you were a boiler maker you learned to lip read – that was the only way we could sometimes communicate. It took several hours to get back to normal hearing afterwards.'

'Another man lost his eye'

This was a commonly used almost casual remark as, in some trades, the possibility of 'losing an eye' was an everyday possibility; boilermakers were particularly vulnerable. So commonplace was the injury that the Medical Fund had an arrangement with a London eye hospital:

ACCIDENT IN THE WORKS

A lad named Nunn, who has only been at work for a short-time, met with a terrible accident on Tuesday while at work in a fitting shop in the GWR Works, a piece of metal chipping striking him in the face and knocking an eye out. Nunn was immediately taken to an eye hospital in London.

Gloucester Citizen, Thursday 21 August 1890

Another claimant for the Workman's Compensation Act Alfred John Barden, a boilermakers' apprentice, claimed compensation at the rate of 6s 8d per week from the GWR Co ... for the loss of his eye occasioned by an accident at his work ... the Company admitted liability for the amounts claimed ... it being understood that the Railway would provide the injured man with work at the same rate of wages as at the time of the accident.

Gloucester Citizen, Wednesday 25 April 1900

Whilst later, in the twentieth century, protective goggles were issued, they did not find favour with the men. The first issue were highly dangerous in themselves as, not only did they create a perfect environment for breeding infections in the eye, they also shattered into pieces when hit by flying objects, so much so that the Company had problems getting the men to try the second, safer, issue:

April 1912 to Company Servants Affected – Goggles

It is generally thought that the new pattern goggles made of wire gauge with a glass front is dangerous owing to the risk of breakage of the glass. This is not so, however, as the glass even though it breaks, retards the speed of the chip and allows the eyelid time to close, thus preventing anything entering the eye, so that not even the broken glass does any damage.

I am sending you a case containing a number of goggles which have been struck by chips. In none of these circumstances was any damage whatsoever done to the eye, but in all of them the sight would have been lost if goggles had not been worn. Please have this case exhibited in a prominent position in your shop for one day and let it be known that goggles can always be obtained by application to the foreman.

Please hand a copy of this circular to each of your chargemen. Sigd CBC

RUSHED TO LONDON HOSPITAL
EXPRESS TRAIN STOPPED AT SWINDON

A GWR express train was deliberately stopped at Swindon in order to rush a GWR employee to the London Eye Hospital. The victim of the accident was Edgar Howell employed … in the riveting shop. A red hot rivet flew up and struck his eye and although treated with all speed at the GWR hospital, the injury was so serious it was considered necessary to send him to London. … It transpired he underwent an immediate operation and has lost the use of one eye.

Western Daily Press and Bristol Mirror,
Monday 17 September 1934

In the GWR Accident Record Book for the 1930s there are many citing different eye injuries. One such in January 1939 is for fitter's apprentice, J.W.P. Hayward, in 15 Shop. The Report states:

As he was walking across the shop a piece of steel flew off a steel bar which was being turned on a lathe, and struck him on the left eye. – Left eye burnt.

Skin

One of the lesser talked about but still significant health problems in the Works was persistent skin complications due to reactions to products such as oil and varnish and swarfe, despite the barrier cream issued for protection. Many men and women suffered irritations and dermatitis, on hands and arms, creating real difficulties.

Mrs Alice Coale – Second World War recruit:

I first worked in B Shop varnishing shell cases. I got dermatitis from it. We had to varnish lots of shells all day. At the end of the day we used paraffin to get the varnish off our hands. After working there for a while I came out all in spots, all over my hands and up my arms. I went to the doctor's and he said it was something in the paraffin didn't agree with me. I was off work on the club for three weeks. I had dermatitis off and on for years after that … had to go into hospital once 'cos it was all over me. Dr Bennet said I could go back to the factory, but not to the same Shop.

Roger Hayes:

When they were cleaning the diesels, the power units, the contaminated oil would get all over their hands. There are a lot of detergents in oil and they would get into the skin and irritate and inflame it. The lanolin cream treatment wasn't always helpful and some men had to be transferred off to other jobs; some even moved into clerical work because their skin would not recover.

Tony Sharkey – Boilermaker:

The only time in my life I have had boils was when I worked 'Inside' mostly in L2 shop. Apparently I was allergic to one of the oils in the factory. I once had a carbuncle which was a big domed boil surrounded by other boils. The nurse at the Centre took pride in popping them all and cleaning it up – horrendous.

Mesothelioma: 'The Swindon Disease'

Mesothelioma is a terminal condition and can be caused by exposure to just one single asbestos fibre. Other asbestos-related diseases include asbestosis, pleural thickening and lung cancer, all of which can be extremely debilitating and life-threatening. It can take many years for an asbestos related illness to develop. Not everyone exposed to it will suffer from an asbestos-related illness but so prevalent was this in the town it became known locally as 'The Swindon disease'. Many of the Works' men were exposed directly or indirectly to asbestos and asbestos dust during their employment with both the Great Western Railway and latterly British Rail.

THE NOT-SO-GOOD BITS

Asbestos (chrysolite), or 'the white dust' or 'fluff' as it was called, is a natural mineral rock with a fibrous nature. Introduced into the Works in the 1930s to coat locomotive boilers for insulation and fire proofing and later used in carriages, too, where it was sprayed on for insulation, it was a part of everyday working life in the factory, in both Works, both in the putting it on and in the taking it off, as this example from a claimant against British Rail vividly shows:

Between 1960–1965 our client was employed by the Defendant as an apprentice coach finisher and body-maker in the Carriage & Wagon Works, Swindon.

Our client stripped fixtures out of carriages which had been sprayed with asbestos. He stripped asbestos insulation from cooking areas in restaurant cars. He was present when woodworking machinists cut asbestos sheets and when labourers brushed up asbestos dust. He fixed and fitted asbestos sheets. He removed asbestos panels from carriages. All of the above work produced substantial amounts of asbestos dust which our client breathed in. He was not provided with nor did he wear respiratory protective equipment.

Mike White:

It was even worse when they brought the boilers back in for stripping down, because when they took off the cleating the hardened asbestos coating would fall off or had to be knocked off and it would rise up in the air like clouds of dust. Even men in the AM Shop, who hadn't even worked with it, died from it, as the clouds of dust would blow through into their shop and they would be breathing it in.

The dust and fibres got everywhere – in your clothes, in your hair, in your nose and mouth and, unhappily, in your lungs. Initially the hidden dangers of this substance were unknown and men worked, and apprentices played, happily with the product. They would lark around having snow-ball fights with it, or push their mates into the heaped up piles.

Later, in the 1950s and '60s, a blue asbestos (crocidolite) was introduced. With its shorter needle-like fibres it is considered by far the most dangerous type and a voluntary ban was placed on it in the 1970s.

The first 'asbestos removal building', as it was documented on Works' plans, was proposed in 1966 and activated in 1968. It was a small affair adjacent to the Spring Shop under Mechanical Services. Later, in 1972, with awareness of the problem growing this now named Asbestos House was altered for 'Wet Suits' and in 1976 it was proposed to extend this facility further. In 1977, however, as the problems became even more recognised, a new 'state-of-the-art' Asbestos House was constructed in the ex-locomotive reception or Receiving Depot area, opposite 25 shop (originally A shop). Whilst this is identified as a 'Dry' unit on Works plans, extensive drainage systems were laid down for the wet room and proper wash-down facilities. This facility was extended in 1980, then the men had protective everything, but by then the damage had already been done.

The top 'fluff house' was still used right up to Works closure; it dealt with all of the smaller jobs. The big fluff house was used for the full strip down jobs or if fluff was found when scraping off the 'black jack'. Ironically this was a popular job for the men as the work was well paid. It engendered an even greater *esprit de corps* and it appealed to their crazy sense of humour to 'dress up like astronauts'.

Unhappily the consequence of decades of asbestos exposure was to cause the death or blighting of later lives of many of Swindon Works' railwaymen and their wives. As one railwayman's wife said: 'If we only knew then, what we know now, it would have saved a lot of heartache.'

DID YOU KNOW?

Works' Mad Rush

Locals knew to be indoors or out of the way when work finished and the men left for home, especially when under pressure of a time constraint at lunchtime. The thunder of feet heralded the 'Works' Mad Rush'. It was a physical phenomenon when thousands of men (14,000 in its heyday), converged into the streets around the Works. It was an impressive sight this 'mass of men' surging down Rodborne Road, as demonstrated in the picture above.

There was a serious chance of mishap as people pushed and shoved their way to the entrances or through the tunnel, the Works main entrance, into Bristol Street and London Road. Female staff were allowed to arrive later and leave a little earlier to avoid this body-squash to 'protect their moral welfare'. Even the men had to take care during the rush, as a memorial dated 17 March 1891 shows:

Application on behalf of John Millard Sadler, Loco Dept. Swindon Works.

Application has been made for assistance from the Company on behalf of John Millar, who is nearly 75 years of age, who has been in the Company's service for about 49 years.

▶ On the 29 July last, as Millard was leaving the Works at 1.0 p.m. he was knocked down by the men rushing out of the shops on either side of him and his thigh was broken. He has not worked since, nor will ever be able to work again.

Many decades later there was anxiety of another kind.

Ian Williams:
Everyone in Swindon centre would get anxious around 4.30 p.m. if they had to travel down Sheppard Street in a car because all the rail workers would descend out of the entrance and pretty much take up all the room on the pavement and road for the next 20 minutes.

DID YOU KNOW?

Clubs
Clubs were a popular feature of the Works. Each shop and office had its own club, which came with its own set of rules and conditions – the more outrageous, the more fun they gave.

Jack Hayward remembers that, in the Wages Office (circa 1960s), theirs was the 'Winkle Club'. Each member had to always carry a winkle shell around with them and, whenever accosted by another member demanding them to 'flash', whether in public or in private, they had to produce their winkle from about their person! Failure to do so resulted in a fine. The fines would be collected by the club secretary, 'Pancho' Reg Haines, so called because of his stocky Mexican looks, and shared out on TRIP, Office outings or at Christmas.

Closure

There were actually *two* closures in the history of the Works, that of the Carriage & Wagon Department in 1967, and the official closure of the remaining Works in March 1986, although, in effect, it took many more months into the following year before everything was finalised.

1967

After the transferring of what remained of the C & W operations across to amalgamate with the Loco Works on 30 June 1967, 'the keys' to the C & W Works were handed to Swindon Corporation on the transfer of ownership of land and property. This area would be demolished and redeveloped to become the Hawksworth Industrial Estate.

JOIN THE FIGHT TO DEFEND THE RAIL WORKS

MARCH & RALLY FRIDAY 21 JUNE

Assemble 1.15. p.m.
West Gate Rodbourne Road

MARCH THROUGH TOWN TO RALLY IN FARINGDON ROAD PARK

RAY BUCKTON   GEN. SEC. A.S.L.E.F.

JIMMY KNAPP   GEN. SEC. N.U.R.

GWYNETH DUNWOODY   M.P. SHADOW SPOKESPERSON ON TRANSPORT

MALCOLM SARGEANT   DEPUTY LEADER THAMESDOWN BOROUGH COUNCIL

GIVE US YOUR SUPPORT

March organised by the Joint Works/Action Committee, Swindon BREL Works.
Leaflet sponsored by Thamesdown Borough Council Rail Works Defence Campaign.

Rail Works Defence Campaign

SAVE THE WORKS

FESTIVAL

FARINGDON ROAD PARK

SATURDAY 20 JULY 12.30.-5

LOTS OF GROUPS AND ORGANISATIONS WILL BE PUTTING ON STALLS OR DISPLAYS....IT'S NOT TOO LATE TO BOOK YOUR FREE SITE...TEL:26161 x3052

THE GATHERING WILL BE ADDRESSED BY PETER SNAPE M.P.

Games, Stalls, Inflatables
Music, Food & Drink

FROM..... * CHARRED HEARTS * * TEDDY WHITE & THE POPULAR BOY CROONERS * UNMISTAKABLE PAUL COOK AND THE LUCKY ONES * * HAMSTERS FROM HELL *

SWINDON WORKS

KEEP IT!

Join the Fight to Defend Rail Workshops

1986

Death of the Railworks: BR just won't Budge over Death Sentence

British rail bosses showed no mercy to the Swindon works. Railwayman Dave McVeigh said:

> We haven't got much chance now – we have been well and truly stitched up – we followed Danny Lee like lambs to the slaughter.

BLACK WEDNESDAY CASTS A SHADOW OVER MR BRUNEL'S RAILWAY WORKS

DAY THAT BRITISH RAIL BLEW THE WHISTLE ON SWINDON

TEARS AS RAILWAY WORKS CLOSES

Tears mixed with bitterness marked the end of Swindon railworks as 1,100 people marched through the gates for the last time.

Many of the railwaymen know they will never work again. For them, Swindon without its rail workshops, will never be the same.

Secretary of the Works' Committee, Terry Larkham wore a black tie which spoke volumes about how he and the men felt. 'This is a funeral,' he told *The Swindon Advertiser.* 'The death of the Works. All are heart broken and bitter because we had proved there was no reason to close us down.'

Evening Advertiser, Wednesday 26 March 1986

Ron Bateman:

> Ultimately, I reached a point when I could no longer stand the sorrowful atmosphere of the place and had to get out. I gathered up a couple of colleagues who felt the same way and we wondered off through the tunnel and went into the Wild Deer on Westcott Place, and there we stayed until closing time.

Eventually I arrived home to a house filled with the sound of children playing and my wife vacuuming and sat staring into space for several minutes, trying to come to accept the realisation that I would never again see the inside of that mighty 'A' Shop. It was a very sad day.

The BREL flag flew at half mast as did the flag on St Mark's church tower. There would be no more Swindon Works' railwaymen.

DEATH OF THE RAIL WORKS

Memories are all that's left for the men who lost their jobs when Swindon railworks closed … .

Evening Advertiser, Saturday 29 March 1986

TARMAC Properties became the new owner.

1987

A small team was retained to do the 'close down'.

BRITISH RAIL ENGINEERING LIMITED.
SWINDON WORKS.
Specially convened Management Structure at the time of closure

John Woodman	Works' Manager
John Walters	Technical Services Manager (Drawing Office, Plant and Machinery, Utility Services)
Maurice Neate (H.Q.)	Chief Accountant
Bill Jefferies	Chief Clerk (Accounts, Stores Controller)
Ken Tanner	Personnel Manager
Bill Bailey	Production Manager

Friday 31 July 1987
'close down' completed
Swindon Railway Works is no more

IN THE WORDS OF THOSE WHO WERE THERE

Edward Snell (1848):

When I was twenty one I calculated on making a fortune by the time I was thirty, but have made little headway ... work getting slacker and slacker ... the men making only four and a half days a week and a great number of them sacked.

Edward Snell was Chief Draughtsman at Swindon and acted as Works' Manager when Archibald Sturrock left in 1850. It was Snell who produced the now famous aerial paintings of Swindon Works in 1846–49.

The Working Men of Swindon Works (1872):

Gentlemen, we the undersigned employees at Swindon works, do most respectfully lay our memorial before you, soliciting that you would grant to us, owing to the very high price of provisions and other accessories of life, ten percent to our day wages and piecework prices.

Your Memorialists would also, Gentlemen, most respectfully ask you, knowing the extra nourishment required to serve a man working overtime, to grant time and a quarter for the first two hours, time and a half for all hours afterwards. Sundays, Christmas Day and Good Friday to be paid double time as was the original custom here.

By granting this request, we remain Gentlemen, your most respectful and obedient servants.

Unfortunately, not granted.

Alfred Williams (1915):

Tuesday is the strong day, the day of vigorous activity, of tool and also of record-breaking. The men come to work like lions. All the stiffness and sluggishness contracted at the weekend has vanished now. There is a great change, both in the temper and the physical condition of the men visible about the place; they move more quickly, handle their tools better, and appear to be in perfect trim. Everyone, from the foreman to the office-boy seems brighter and better, more fit, well and energetic – great things are accomplished on Tuesdays at the works.

Foreman's Diary, 11 April 1919:

Erectors V Boilermakers. Cab.4700. Because the boilermakers bolted the bottom of the side plates where previously riveted, cleaders (Reeves) was instructed by shop steward and committee to cease work on cab weather board etc. I notified Mr Collett, who called for G Davis and H Watkins to settle same. Final meeting held in AE Shop Office at which Mr Watkins (foreman), H Watkins for Boilermakers, J Pearce Boilermaker Shop Steward, G Davis A&E, F Drinkwater Erector Shop Steward, S Thomas Cost Office, and myself were present. Agreed on this cab – Boilermakers bolt bottom of side plates and cab top on, cleaders bolt weather board and leg plates. Unions to discuss future iron cabs.

(A verbatim transcription of serial manuscript entries in a 'Boots Scribbling Diary' for the year 1918, found in the office of A shop and preserved by G.D. Neate)

Trevor Cockbill, author of *Finest Thing Out***:**

Most of our fathers worked 'Inside' ... and most of us expected to work in the railway factory too when our time came. The thought of it was not desirable, nor objectionable, but logical, inevitable for each of us.

Frank Saunders:

It was mapped out for you, people knew. The teacher would say 'Where are you going to work?' 'Inside' that's what you'd say, 'Inside the railway.' 'Right, what are you going to be?' 'Oh, I don't know, Sir.' 'Well, what's your father?' 'He's a machinist.' 'Well you can be a machinist.' Your father would go over to the Manager's Office or see the foremen and that would be it.' Try as they might, no matter how quick or academically bright they might be, the boys could not 'buck the system'. They had to knuckle-down and accept or seek their fortune elsewhere. This was expected and accepted thinking but, however expected it was, many a young lad's hopes and dreams for other things were dashed by this excessive control.

John Attwell (1930s):

The Works had big walls all around, not just to keep people from getting in but to stop the workers getting out. Each entrance had a gateman and to leave you had to have a pass-out slip.

Violet Lane (1930s):

When I started work we were expected to dress in an acceptable way, wear skirts of a suitable length, that is two inches below the knee and sandals were definitely not allowed. I know of one girl who was sent up to the Chief Clerk because she hadn't dressed properly and another girl who came in sandals was sent as well. Trousers were unheard of. In fact I never saw them in all my time there which was up to 1960. When I started I used to earn 12/6d a week and I was very pleased with it.

WORDS OF THOSE WHO WERE THERE

Diane Fitchett (1970s):

I was sixteen and applying for my first job at the Job Centre in Swindon Town. They sent me straight up to the Works. I remember it well as I was wearing desert boots, flares and a t-shirt. I felt very much a young and with-it teenager. You can imagine then that I was very taken aback when at the end of interview Mrs. Benson, the [Telephone] Exchange Supervisor said to me that I had got the job but would I please wear a *frock* when I started. *A FROCK!!* That one word summed up just how old-fashioned it was in there. We would never dare call Mrs. Benson by her Christian name; it would not have been allowed, far too familiar. Not only did we have to watch what we wore, but what we said and how we behaved. I was a normal lively teenager and everyone else seemed so much older and part of the furniture. It seemed very old-fashioned and strict to me, far more strict than the school I had just left.

Dr Barbara Carter (1940s):

There was great camaraderie amongst the girls. When we had a 21st birthday or Wedding Eve the person's desk was decorated and everyone wrote a poem about you and it was put on the board around your desk; they were usually made to embarrass you!! I still have mine. On your last day you were allowed to leave a minute early so that you could be 'banged' out. All your friends got hold of a heavy ruler or a tin and BANGED the desks HARD. As your office started so others along the way took it up and you had to 'run the gauntlet' of a terrific din.

Henry J. Smith: (1930s–'40s):

For me, as a young teenager, Q Shop, where the angle-ironsmiths, plied their trade amid the forges, furnaces, flames and fumes, not to mention heat, sparks and sweat, was another world, a wonderland. Everything on an engine that required angle-iron was fashioned and formed here. I especially loved the way the sparks flew everywhere. The men wore some protective sacking, especially on their forearms, but us young lads didn't. We liked to get our arms burned so that when we went out we could 'show off' how hard our work was and how hard we were!

Another fascinating place was W Shop, full of a wide range of machinery on which a wide variety of machining was done such as the boring of the huge cylinders. They were big. Then, everything was hand done, even boring to a 1,000th of an inch. Those machinists, working on hand-made machines that were already ancient, decades old, were so expert, they instinctively knew when the required 'tho had arrived and shouted out and tapped the machine with a spanner declaring it.

Cyril Godwin (1940s):

I finished my apprenticeship in 1939 just when war broke out. All the apprentices that were finishing about that time they had over in the offices and asked for volunteers for the Royal Engineer Company, the Workshops' company they were making up, and I volunteered as I wanted to get in the railway workshops company, rather than any other one, that way I knew my job was protected when I came back after the war. At the end of the war I went back into coppersmithing. The Unions got us all back on the books.

Roy Blackford (1944):

I was a Coach Finisher. A first class trade. All the years I worked for the railway I worked on everything from horse boxes to royal saloons, things like that. It was wonderful work. A wonderful trade. A lot of it was handcrafted in those days.

The types of timber we had down in the Saw Mill, were mahogany, ash, beech, wet oak, rough oak. Most of it before the war was brought in from overseas. The GWR didn't buy bits and pieces in B & Q like, they would buy a shipload of timber.

It would go into the No 1 Shop that was over the Loco side – still part of the C side, be cut down into planks, then it would be stored down at Newburn, in racks and dried. You'd have racks and racks of this timber with all the dates on and they'd only use it after it had been there so many years. Kiln dried wasn't heard of then.

A lot of the good timber was used up during the war. When I started in 2 shop in 1944, in 4 Shop they were making Chariots, the two men submarines, where they sat astride, they were actually building them in there. These Chariots were stood up on trestles where they were being worked on and a lot of the mahogany they had in store was being used for that.

Ernie Fischer (1946–1986):

My grandfather was a boiler maker … he worked on the splashes that went under the *Great Bear*. It was a one off, a huge locomotive. Apparently there was a fault in the drawing and when they made these splashes they wouldn't fit. He was so worried about it he couldn't eat his dinner just sat and worried about it, but it turned out it was a fault in the drawing. So he was let off. (Poor Mr Fischer he was probably thinking of the Rules and Regulations No 21 which states; 'Any workman making an article of wrong dimension … , may be called upon to make good such work and be liable to a fine of 2s 6d or to instant dismissal.' Such a worry would put anyone off their dinner.)

Peggy Pinnegar (1949–early '50s):

I have lots of good memories of F shop. I was very happy. Lots of friendship. If the blacksmith did something wrong like, all the others would cheer and shout. We'd all help each other. I had worked in Wills factory before. It was very strict in there. Going 'Inside' it was a lot more easy. We were on a man's wage. £8.90. A flat rate. No bonus. I worked at the aircraft factory previous to that for £4.50 so that was the difference. A man's job for a man's wage and a Free Pass, of course. That was the incentive to go 'Inside'.

Jack Hayward:

I started my clerical life in J1 Shop office in 1956. I can remember my friend, Ernie Edwards, who already worked Inside, advising me against my choice of employment adding that The Works was due for closure with no future. My parents said I had a job for life. Indeed that was the perceived wisdom at the time. As things turned out I suppose I did but what a roller coaster ride it was; one reorganisation followed by another. We suffered amalgamations, assimilations, rationalisation, but they all added up to staff redundancies and a reduction in the number of posts.

My first experience of reorganisation was being transferred from the Ledger Office to the Stores Accounts Office in 1962. A year later another reorganisation saw me placed in the Chief Accountants Office. In 1964 my post was declared redundant and I relocated to the Cost Accounts Office. After yet another upheaval I landed up in the Estimates and Tenders Office. 1968 found me posted as Assistant Works Cashier and two years later I found myself in the Central Wages Office, it was here that I witnessed the turmoil of our currency conversion from Imperial to Decimal. I remained in this post until finally it was announced that the Works was to close in March 1986. It was a huge shock. I made up my mind to leave the Works for pastures new in 1985.

My starting salary on entering Swindon Works was £350 per year, while my exit salary was £10,120 per year.

Ken White (Sign painter, 1958):

I was the first apprentice they'd had for years. Fifteen or twenty. I was something of a novelty. It was a bit overwhelming, being seventeen and all the other blokes being so much older. First thing was to make my own palette. I was given some plywood. I enjoyed that. Made it real artistic like. Not just a square with a whole in. I was proud of that. Still got it in fact. In my studio. I started on stencilling. They provided the stencilling brushes. They were named after birds. Still are. Depending on their size. Goose. Swan. Duck. They had to be cleaned and laid in a dish of oil every night to keep them in good condition. Every morning we would go up 'the Bank' and do touch-up of old work. Go over the work already done to bring it back up. Do whole letters. I did that for about a year.

Roger Hayes (1950s–'60s):

It was an exciting time to be in the Works then. Lots of changes taking place. We were very enthusiastic. It was exciting because we were handling German locomotives called Maybachs. They were really one of the best. Two or three German engineers came over from Germany to Swindon to work with us. There was a lot of interest but there was a certain element of unease by some workmen, certainly the older ones. They found it a bit difficult. They were older, knew steam and were not used to diesels and, of course, the war was not long gone, so not everyone was happy to be working with Germans in the factory. All the u-boats had had the same engines that we had in our trains, but it was alright. They helped us and it was part of the regeneration of Germany after the war. Western Region was picked out to try these new locomotives. We built the locomotive in Swindon Works. The engines were made by Rolls Royce under licence. The Maybachs were very successful locomotives. Sadly when British Rail wanted to standardise, these were the locos they did away with.

Pat Sullivan (1960s):

When I was a fully-fledged tradesman I worked on the early diesels. The 6300s. We'd do a general repair. Strip everything out. The engine would go to the B shed or the 9 Shop. The transmission would go to AM shop. All the electrical gear would go to the E shop and that would all be re-furbished. The pipe work would go back to the coppersmith and that would all be repaired. Everything would go away to the different people. And then you'd clean everything up, repair what needed to be repaired and put everything back again. When it was *finished* you would go on trial with it. That was a nice part.

Jim Rogers:

In the 1970s my trade almost died out. I got sent down the Con Yard burning up old wagons for scrap. After a year of that I got drafted on to a boilermaking job, then I had four years in the Saw-Mill, then back on the boilermaking activity until the Works closed.

Bob Townsend (1970s):

About a year before I left, more and more people were being made redundant. It was a matter of last in first out ... so what happened was, because there were chaps down in A Shop who had been in longer than I and my colleagues had, they sent up those men in A shop so we could teach them to do our jobs and then we were sent to AM Shop. I ended up on the Webster and Bennet Vertical boring machine, machining axleboxes working on nights. I worked mainly nights. I volunteered because you got more money on nights. Then 31 December 1972 it was out the door. We knew for a while that we were going that day. Not a good way to start the New Year. It was quite depressing. I got redundancy payment about £325. It was not that good. A few weeks pay. I think I was earning between £20–£28 per week at that time. Today youngsters lose their jobs and move around all the time, but in those days, when we went into the railway we thought we went in for life. However, looking back I think I'm glad I was forced out. At the time with a mortgage and two kids it was cause for concern. I couldn't get a job for three to four month as Pressed Steel didn't have any vacancies, but I think it was for the good, for me.

Richard O'Keefe:

For someone who did not know Swindon before I went there in 1975 to the Works Apprentice Training School, the lasting impression was the high level of skill of the men that came off the Works shop floor to share their knowledge and skill with us fresh faced youths. Their motto was – *there is everyone else's way and then there is the Swindon way* – the Swindon way being a higher quality and standard.

Gordon Dickinson (1976):

The training school was connected to the Works by an underground tunnel. Toward the end of the year it was announced that we would be going through the tunnel and emerge in the 'real world' for a tour of what was to become our work place for at least the next four years. This, for me, was probably the most exciting day of my whole apprenticeship.

We were then taken to where we would be working to meet our new 'mates' this was the point I realised that I had chosen the right trade. These men were in contrast to most of the others clean and fairly tidy, a lot of them (the finishing gang) were wearing collar and ties, not too much sweat was in evidence and it all seemed quite civilised, these people were known as 'the silver arsed gang' … that was what I decided I was going to become. Although there was something in the way they looked at us, with an almost devilish wryness, that made me feel slightly wary of what was in store for us … as we stood there, dressed in our sparkling clean green (very apt) overalls the expression 'fresh meat' entered my head.

Michael Midge Madden (1970s):

Most memorable thing? Getting thrown into the wash basins as an apprentice on an almost daily basis!

Ron Bateman:

I entered the WTS in September 1977 and went 'down the slope' on Black Wednesday 1986. I was a coach painter 19 Shop/19A Shop. Engine painter (26 shop) and had two spells in 'D' Shop (Maintenance painter). My Magnificent 7 of the Works would be – 1. The Men; 2. The mighty 'A' Shop; 3. The Hooter; 4. Shared vocabulary; 5. The training programme; 6. The Traversing Tables & cranes; 7. The Black Pay Tables.

Harry Roberts (1970s):

My own arrival as Works' Manager in July 1972 was not exactly heralded with a fanfare of trumpets as it was an open secret that my remit was to close the Works down completely, the quicker the better so far as the Board were concerned. … The actual timing of when the poacher decided to turn gamekeeper is difficult to define. Subconsciously, no doubt, I had been absorbing the true potential obscured under the disorientated, demoralised atmosphere which pervaded the Works. …

I consulted with my principal assistants on the feasibility of developing an economic survival plan for the Works. The leeway to be made up was truly horrendous in magnitude, but it was agreed that 'nothing ventured nothing gained' …

The corporate plan was based on the simple philosophy of 'more output from a reduced space, with less men at the right price, to the prescribed quality within the scheduled time period'. …

It is appropriate I think that the first locomotive, the *Great Western*, and the last to be built at Swindon, were both completed in record-breaking times. The common factor to both instances was the superb quality and dedication of the Swindon craftsmen and I am very proud of the fact that for nearly a decade I had the privilege of working with such men as their Works' Manager.

Malcolm Holland:

After finishing my time I was allocated a fitter's position in 19 shop, once again with Dave Middleton as my charge-hand. This time however, I was the lowest of the low, a new boy and it was off to the lift roads, the dirtiest filthiest area of 19 shop (originally the B shed) which had the job of overhauling DMU's (Diesel Multiple Unit) cars. Units would arrive in the shop on a Monday morning, be lifted off their bogies, have all mechanical components removed and replaced or overhauled depending on Inspectors' reports and be finished by Friday morning to be moved to the test roads to be prepared for returning to service. In amongst all this other deeper body refurbishments and repaints had to be scheduled in and catered for. Many of these units had been in service for at least three years since their last major overhaul, so the undersides were foul, oil, grease and in the days before toilet holding tanks, a lot of other stuff. This was the job that greeted us every Monday morning. We had our clean overalls provided on a Monday morning and usually by mid- morning break we were soaked in oil and diesel and covered in other stuff!

During my time on the gang I saw things become more and more difficult. Spares were often not available resulting in units leaving the lift roads, often without essential parts, that then had to be fitted in the far more difficult surroundings of the test roads. This tended to cause a degree of hostility between the two sections of the gang, with the perception that we, on the lift roads, were in some way slacking on our duties – we couldn't fit what we didn't have!

WORDS OF THOSE WHO WERE THERE

John 'Jack' Fleetwood:

I started work in the 'Scraggery' when I was fifteen years old, facing off nuts and putting threads in them. After one year I was taken to the Iron Foundry to start my trade as a 'Moulder, Iron & Brass'. When I entered the doors at the end of the foundry, it frightened me to death. It was big, dirty, and hot, as it was July. It was known as one of the 'hot shops' and was it hot – hot in the summer and freezing cold in the winter as there was no heating in the shop, except in the foreman's and clerks' office. When I asked if we could have some heating in the shop, I was told by the foreman: 'Work a bit harder and you will get warm!'

The work was very heavy, and dangerous. There were often accidents, little ones and serious ones. As regards safety in our shop it was poor and sparse. We did get issued with protective goggles, all metal with window glass in the lens. It would shatter if you dropped them on the floor – ha ha, not great for eyes, and they gave us styes. They issued leather spats to protect the ladle runners' feet. We used to turn the hosepipe on our boots if the molten iron went through the eyelets. Hard it was, but great memories.

Ian Williams:

To be honest, the railworks was one huge storybook where almost everyone knew everyone someway or other, and if you were on your own anywhere in the town, in a pub or club, cafe or bar, there would always be someone else who recognised you from 'the Works' and came across and chatted to you, so in a manner of speaking if you worked in the Works, you would never be alone wherever you went in the town.

Alan Lambourne (1986):

Finally, I suppose, I am a living example of that old Swindon adage, 'Once a railwayman, always a railwayman!'

TIMELINE AND MILESTONES

1840   **6 October** the GWR Board of Directors resolved 'that the principal locomotive and repairing shops be established at, or near, the junction with the Cheltenham and Great Western Union at Swindon.'

1841   **25 February** the GWR Board agreed to build 'a depot' where 'a change of engine may be advantageously made. … The establishment would also comprehend the large repairing shops for the Locomotive department.'
20 April the GWR Board voted £34,290 for its construction.

1842   **November** – machinery started up.

1843   **2 January** – the Works opened for full-time business.

1846   **February** – build begins of 'Premier' Class 1st Lot Goods – (up until then it was a repair and maintenance depot). *Premier,* is the first in this class and the first engine to be built at Swindon (but with a boiler bought in from Stephenson). *Jason* is the 12th and last engine in this series, built May 1847.

1 April – Daniel Gooch's Broad Gauge *Great Western* – the first engine to be *totally* built by the Company at the Works, completed and 'steamed'. The Gauge Commissioners report in favour of the 'narrow' gauge 4ft 8½in. This becomes the 'standard' gauge for all new railways.

1847 **GWR Medical Fund** started – it will grow into the most amazing service from 'the cradle to the grave'.

1848 **14 June – TRIP** commenced – a day trip to Oxford that eventually led to a two-week, paid annual holiday and becomes part of the Works' legend.

1849 **December** – After a financial review GWR Board ordered four weighbridges to be constructed at the Works for the use of the Company. The start of doing things in-house, the end of contractors.

1850 **Standardised goods wagons** begin to be produced.

1855 **First 'narrow' gauge 0-6-0 engine No. 57 Class** built in the Works.

1861 **Rolling Mill** built and managed by William Ellis. Later he became Chief Inspector of Rails for the Permanent Way Department.

1864 Daniel Gooch resigns and is succeeded by Joseph Armstrong.

1868 Building of **Carriage Works** begins.

1869 Latter part of year first coaching stock goes into service. This was for standard gauge traffic, not until

1874 did they build broad gauge stock. The Works now had three principal departments: the Locomotive works, which were situated in the fork between the main line to Bristol and the branch line to Gloucester; the Carriage works on the south side to the main line to Bristol; and the Wagon works, north of the main line and east of the Gloucester line.

1871   Construction of Water Tower:

For some months past workmen have been employed in putting up a queer-looking erection at the south-west corner of the carriage shed. It consists of several tiers of large long iron columns standing on each other about twenty-five feet square. On top of this framework there will be a water tank. Connected immediately with this tank there will be pipes running through and around the inside of the carriage works. In the tank there will be kept a constant supply of fifty thousand gallons of water. Meanwhile ... twelve portable fire extinguishers are kept in constant readiness over the shops.

The Swindon Advertiser, 8 March

NOTICE

Commencing December 25th 1871 the 9 Hour System was adopted, 54 hours per week constituting a full weeks work. signed by *W Armstrong*.

The men celebrated with a Parade through the town. At this time weekly wages (rather than fortnightly) were introduced to help alleviate difficulties from the wage cuts for fewer hours.

From 1872 to 1876, considerable expansion of the Works took place including a new Boiler Shop (V shop) and an extension that became the Tender Shop.

1874   New Royal Saloon incorporating body parts from 1852 completed. This was later converted to standard gauge. The first all-female workshop opened in the C & W Dept.

1877   Joseph Armstrong died suddenly and was replaced by
William Dean.

1878   Work began on new separate **Carriage and Wagon** Works
built on land north of the station.
Rail Mill no longer produces rails but works on as a
Rolling Mill.

No new engines were ordered between **March 1883** and **August
1887** (except four experimental prototypes – No. 7, No. 8, No 10.
and No 13. Two reasons for this. Armstrong's excellent engines
made none necessary and the Great Depression was biting hard.

1889   **February** – 105 special trucks for agricultural machinery
and fish, meat, and poultry vans ordered – climb back from
depression begins.

Between **January 1891** and **February 1892** narrow-gauge rolling
stock worth £628,270 was ordered – all constructed at the Works,
although some parts bought in.

1892   **7 March** – GWR introduced a new set of coaches on its
Paddington to Birkenhead service. Designed by Dean, it
was the first British side-corridor train where a corridor
connection was provided between all the coaches.

1895   Massive investment in re-equipping workshops began.

1892   End of the Broad Gauge era. The date of the final track
conversion — a wonderful feat of engineering — carried
out on 21 and 22 May. The Works becomes BG graveyard.
All broad gauge engines, wagons and coaches (with the
exception of a few hundred wagons which were taken into
the Bridgwater Shops) came to Swindon for conversion

to narrow-gauge or for breaking up. Thirteen miles of additional sidings were laid down for their reception. When the work of conversion was at its height, the number of hands employed in the Swindon Locomotive Works was 5,758, and in the Carriage, Wagon, and Stores Department 4,157; a total of 9,915.

1900   Electric lighting introduced in carriages. New work for Swindon.

1902   William Dean retires and is replaced by George Jackson Churchward.

1903   'Record Breaker' *City of Truro* 3440 built.

1908   **February** – building of ground-breaking Pacific No. 111 *The Great Bear*.

It is surprising to think that in the Edwardian period such a giant was possible, which says much about the technical knowledge of Swindon Works and its workers' abilities. The workers that made this colossus must have been as pleased as punch with it, not only was it a milestone in the great history of this town, but also a benchmark in the annals of railway evolution and now its history.

The Swindon Advertiser, December 2008
(marking No 111's Centenary)

1914–1918 First World War – Works becomes part of the war effort. Women introduced into workshops on munitions work and carriage cleaning.

1916   Locomotive Carriage & Wagon Superintendent title changed to Chief Mechanical Engineer.

TIMELINE AND MILESTONES

1919   **1 January:** Forty-seven-hour week introduced into the Works. The early shift, known as the breakfast shift, is dropped. New hours of work: Monday–Friday, 8.00 a.m.–12.30 p.m./1.30 p.m.–5.30 p.m.; Saturday, 7.30 a.m.–12 noon.

1922   George J. Churchward retires and Charles Benjamin Collett becomes CME.

1923   **1 January** The Railways Act of 1921 (Grouping or Amalgamation Act) came into being creating 'the BIG FOUR'. Only the GWR Company retained its name. A great many 'foreign' (i.e. non-GWR) engines find themselves in Swindon Works for repair and refit or scrapping, depending on condition.

1923   **August** – Introduction of the *Castle* Class locomotives – the *Caerphilly Castle* was put into service.

1926   **March** – The *Western Daily Press* reports that a petition was presented to the House of Commons by Swindon Corporation to permit GWR to establish 'a very large supply of **electricity**' to the Works.

1926   **3 May** – at the end of the working day Swindon Works men rake out their fires in readiness for the official beginning of the 'General Strike' the next day. Later, apprentices join the strike.

1927   Introduction of the *Kings* Class locomotive.

1928   Introduction of 3rd class sleeping cars makes new work for C & W Department.

1929   Annual Report of the Chief Mechanical Engineer for the Year 1929:

NEW CARRIAGE SHOP

The new carriage shop has now the roof on, and has been so far completed as to enable a portion to be utilised. There are already housed in this building some 50 carriages and when it is completed it will accommodated between 200 and 250.

RELIEF OF UNEMPLOYMENT   [Government Funded Scheme]

In connection with the Railway Development Schemes, the old A Shed, which was built in 1846, has been demolished to allow for extension and improvements of the adjoining shops.

1934   New GWR roundel becomes part of the C & W painters' work.
July: The first 'Buffet' car No. 9631 outshopped.

1935   The Great Western Railway Company Centenary. Celebrations involve building two new complete trains for the Cornish Riviera Express.

1938   Works produce the under frames, bogies, brakes and bodies for **AEC 10 ton diesel railcar**.

1939–1945 Second World War – Works again becomes part of the Government's war effort. From December 1942 women between the ages of twenty and thirty years (later extended to forty) were conscripted to war-work and into the Works doing War-work AND railway work.

1941   **March** – The first Swindon version of the diesel railcar No 12 completed.
Collett retired; replaced by Frederick W. Hawksworth.

1943   The **Centenary of the Works** – as taken from when the Works started full-time production. It is the time of the Second World War and wartime demands do not allow time or materials for celebrations.

1947   Prairie 2-6-2 Tank locomotive No. 4150 was built at a cost of £7,400 and entered traffic on 5 June. (Now preserved.)

1948   **1 January – Nationalisation** – the Transport Act of 1947 came into effect, nationalising all British railways. The Great Western Railway Company, which had been in existence for 113 years, was no more. The control of the GWR comes under the new British Transport Commission – the Works comes under British Railway Western Region.

1950   Work starts on first standard railway locos:

These are the first standard design locomotives for use on British Railways and represent two of a possible 12 new standard designs – to be made in the Works.

British Machine Tool Engineering, April–June 1950

1951   First **BR Standard Locomotive of Class 4 75000 4-6-0** built.

1952   British Transport Commission Report suggests the trial use of diesel railcars – good news for the Works.

1956   **January** – permission given for Works to build three pilot **D800 'Warships', D800 – 2**.
Set-up of the **Welding School** to meet Health & Safety requirements, first in K Shop then circa 1960 moved to A Shop.

1957   **February** – order of **30 D800s – with Maybach engines** uprated to 1,135bhp each, except for number D830, which employed Paxman 12YJX engines, though again of 1,135bhp.

1958–61 The **Class 120**, were a cross-country DMU in three-car formation. A total of 194 were built at the Works in three batches.

1958 – 49 sets for the Western Region
1959 – 7 sets for the Scottish Region
1961 – another 9 sets for the Western Region

1958   **August** – First **D800 'Warship'** class, *Sir Brian Robertson*, entered service. Other 'pilots' were *Vanguard* and *Formidable*.

1960   **March** – Last steam locomotive built at Swindon works for British Railways **92220 *Evening Star*** was named at a ceremony in the erecting shop.

1961   Local headline – '**Work Position in Swindon B.R. Factory alarms trade unions. Order for wagons lost to private firm**'.

1961   **December** – Diesel – hydraulic 'Western' series much loved in the Works – D1000 **'Western Enterprise'** entered traffic. It was the first 'Western' to run off the Works' production line and was outshopped in a unique striking desert sand livery with wheels, roof panels, bogies and window frames in black. Buffer beams and front skirts were originally painted in carmine red.

1962   'The Main Workshops Future Plan' – all British Railways Workshops detached from their operating regions and placed under a central authority – **British Railway Workshops** with headquarters at Derby. This does not bode well for Swindon.

1962   First intake into the new Works' **Apprentices Training School** – the beginning of a new era.

1963   **January** – receives order for 26 of **British Rail Class 14**, a type of small diesel-hydraulic 0-6-0 locomotive. Order later increased to 56.

1963 **March** – Dr Beeching's Policy to 'Make the Railways Pay' – A decision was made to specify all new classes of locomotive have diesel-electric transmission, thereby making the Works' specialist diesel-hydraulic knowledge redundant. A big blow for Swindon Works.

1963 Carriage & Wagon Department begins to transfer all its *remaining* activities (some have been lost to other regions) and workmen across to Loco side. Work still continues over the next few years of this happening. Redundancies. All the remaining workshops will (eventually) be concentrated in area formerly occupied by Loco Works, viz 104 acres of which 32 are roofed.

1963 Prototype carriage B 13252.

1964 The last 3 of order for 30 – 2,700hp Type 4 Diesel Hydraulic Class D.1000 Locomotives are released.

SWINDON WORKS REPORT FOR THE FIRST HALF OF 1964

Iron Foundry and Rolling Mill closed. All men from Iron Foundry offered employment within Works, those from the Rolling Mill were offered vacancies on the Western Region. The Laundry, Grease & Oil Works also closed.

1964 **July** – the first of 56 small diesel-hydraulic locomotives, designated as TOPS Class 14 by British Railways, appear from the Works. They become known affectionately by enthusiasts as 'Teddy Bears', following a comment purportedly by Works' foreman George Cole who rued, 'We've built the Great Bear, now we're going to build a Teddy Bear.'

1965 **October** – Last locomotive built for British Rail. Class 14 D9555 650hp diesel hydraulic locomotive was outshopped.

1966   Former Iron Foundry (J1) converted to new Diesel Engine Repair – 9 shop.

1967   Irony – not quite 100 years after opening Carriage & Wagon Works is finally closed. Now just 'the Works'. Number of workshops reduced.
£2.3 million modernisation fund allocated to the Works. Major exodus of staff to other railway centres particularly the new Railway Technical Centre at Derby.

1968   The 125th Anniversary of Locomotive Works and the Centenary of Carriage and Wagon Works.

1970   **1 January** – The 1968 Transport Act brought into being British Rail Engineering Ltd.
Formation of Workshop Company (Boundaries) Committee to identify site, borders, users, ownership and future maintenance of each and every item that traversed 'the border'.
The Works now takes in 'outside' orders for a diverse variety of general engineering jobs.

1979   A new opportunity – order for 20 new-build locomotives for Kenya; these were special metre gauge, 625hp, diesel-hydraulic locomotives, which required new jigs, specialist tools and track provision. Despite severe constraints and against expectations these were delivered on budget, on time.

1980   A small 'resurgence' staff numbers have increased to 3,800.

1985   **February** – BREL announce a continued future for the Works.
May – announcement made to 'close the Works'.
The 150th Anniversary of the GWR – meets a cool reception in the Works and Swindon because of impending imposture.

Centenary of St John's Ambulance Brigade in the Works. (Believed not confirmed, but announced).

December – Inquiry and Review of Closure decision.

1986   **Wednesday 25 March** – Official Works' closure – some personnel remain behind to 'close down'.

1987   **Friday 31 July 1987** departure of few remaining staff. Swindon Works now CLOSED.

'BACK TO THE FUTURE'

Only what can adapt will endure

Swindon's Railway Works closed in 1986. Its buildings then lay empty and derelict. A once noisy and industrious place lay ominously quiet. The 'sound of silence' prevailed.

Yet today Swindon's historic railway area is recognised as an exemplar for the restoration of heritage industrial buildings with a powerful 'sense of place'. The award winning transformation of the Swindon Works is a success story in the rejuvenation of historic industrial sites. In this case 'a phoenix rose from the ashes'. Brunel would be proud of his legacy.

Swindon Borough Council

BIBLIOGRAPHY

Books

Ball, Felicity & Bryan, Tim, *Swindon and the GWR*, Tempus Publishing Ltd, 2003.

Binks, Andy & Timms, Peter, *Swindon Works Through Time*, Amberley Publishing, 2015.

Bryan, Tim, *The Golden Age of the Great Western 1895–1914*, Patrick Stephen, 1991.

Bryan, Tim, *Great Western Swindon*, The Chalford Publishing Company, 1995.

Catell, John & Faulkner, Keith, *Swindon: The Legacy of a Railway Town*, HMSO, 1995.

Cockbill, Trevor, *Finest Thing Out: The Story of the Mechanics' Institute at New Swindon 1843–1873*, The Quill Press, Swindon, 1988.

Cockbill, Trevor, *Our Swindon in 1939*, Quill Press, Swindon, 1989, 2nd Edition, The Mechanics' Institute Preservation Trust Ltd, 1999.

Cook, Kenneth J., *Swindon Steam 1921–1951*, Ian Allan Ltd, 1974.

Crittal, Elizabeth, Rogers, K.H. and Shrimpton, Colin, *A History of Swindon to 1965*, Institute of Historical Research & Wiltshire Library & Museum Service, Trowbridge, 1983. This book was reprinted from *The Victoria History of Wiltshire Volume IX*.

Darwin, Bernard, *A Century of Medical Service: The Story of the Great Western Railway Medical Fund Society 1847 to 1947*, The GWR Medical Fund Society, Swindon, 1947.

Durrant, A.E., *Swindon Apprentice, An Inside Portrait of the Great Western Locomotive Works*, Runpast Publishing, 1989.

Freebury, Hugh, *Great Western Apprentice, Swindon in the Thirties*, Wiltshire County Council Library & Museum Service, 1985.

Gibbs, Ken, *Swindon Works: Apprentice in Steam*, Oxford Publishing Company, 1986.

Gibbs, Ken, *The Steam Locomotive – An Engineering History*, Amberley Press, 2012.

Gibbs, Ken, *The Great Western Railway – How It Grew*, Amberley Press, 2012.

Grinsell L.V. et al, *Studies in the History of Swindon*, Swindon Borough Council, 1950.

Haresnape, Brian and Swain, Alec, *Churchward Locomotives – A Pictorial History*, Ian Allan Ltd, 1976.

Large, Frederick, *A Swindon Retrospect: 1855–1930*, Borough Press, 1932.

Larkin, Edgar, *An Illustrated History of British Railways Workshops*, Oxford Publishing Company, 1992.

Matheson, Dr. Rosa, *TRIP – The Annual Holiday of GWR's Swindon Works*, Tempus Publishing, 2006.

BIBLIOGRAPHY

The Fair Sex – Women and the Great Western Railway, Tempus Publishing, 2007.

Railway Voices 'Inside' Swindon Works, The History Press, 2008.

The GWR Story, The History Press, 2010.

Apprenticeship and Training 'Inside' Swindon Works, The History Press, 2011.

Measom, George, *The Illustrated Guide to The Great Western Railway*, W. Marshall & Sons, 1852.

Morris, William, *Swindon: Reminiscences, Notes and Relics of Ye Old Wiltshire Towne*, 1885.

Mountford, Eric R., *Swindon, GWR Reminiscences*, Bradford Barton Ltd, 1980(?).

Peck, Alan, *The Great Western at Swindon Works*, Oxford Publishing Company, 1983.

Potts, C.R., *The GWR and the General Strike*, The Oakwood Press, 1996.

Platt, Alan, *The Life and Times of Daniel Gooch*, Alan Sutton, 1987.

Tuckett, Angela, *Up With All That's Down: A History of Swindon's Trades Council 1891–1971*, The Quill Press, 2nd edition, 1982.

Wells, H.B., 'John Betjeman, Architecture' in *Studies in the History of Swindon*, L.V. Grinsell et al, Swindon Borough Council, 1950.

Wells, H.B., 'Swindon in the 19th and 20th Centuries' in *Studies in the History of Swindon*, L.V. Grinsell et al, Swindon Borough Council, 1950.

Williams, Alfred, *Life in A Railway Factory*, Duckworth, 1915.

Newspapers

Astill's Swindon Almanac and Trade Guide: New Swindon

Devizes and Wiltshire Gazette

Gloucester Citizen

Reading Mercury

The Swindon Advertiser and North Wilts Chronicle

The Citizen

The Daily Chronicle

The Swindon Advertiser / The Evening Advertiser

The Wiltshire Gazette & Herald

Western Daily Press

Western Times

Magazines and Journals

The Engineer, 1908

British Machine Tool Engineering Vol.xx11 No 160 April–June 1950. 'Swindon Works British Railways Western Region'

The Great Western Railway Magazine

The Railway Correspondence and Travel Society, 1953 'Locomotives of the Great Western Railway Part Two Broad Gauge'

The Railway Gazette

The Railway Journal

Primary Sources

STEAM Museum of the Great Western Railway, Swindon

Swindon Museum and Art Gallery, Swindon

Local Studies, Central Library, Swindon

Wiltshire and Swindon History Centre, Chippenham

Private Collections
Author's own collection
Swindon Society
Newton Abbott Library and Record Centre

Academic Papers and Journals
Brownlee, Mike, 'The Railway Works at Swindon and Stratford in the 19th Century: a comparison of their origins, activity and labour force and their social impact on their respective neighbourhoods.' Master thesis. September 2010
http://sas-space.sas.ac.uk/2812/1/Brownlee_-_MA_dissertation_-_2010.pdf
'Engineering and Railway Works' - A History of the County of Wiltshire: Volume 4. Originally published by Victoria County History, London, 1959. Pages 183-219
www.british-history.ac.uk/vch/wilts/vol4/pp183-219

Articles
Hayward, Jack, 'Swindon' Railway offices Shaped by History', *North Star,* Friends of
  Swindon Railway Museum Newsletter 2001/2
White, A.J.L., 'The Swindon Works'. *The Great Western Railway Magazine* 1915–1927

Memoirs and Monographs
Dumas, Conrad Knowle (unpublished)
Fleetwood, Jack (unpublished)
Harber, Jack (unpublished)
Walter, K. *Swindon Air Raids in World War Two*, published privately 1998

Commemorative Magazines and Booklets
The Town and Works of Swindon with a Brief History of the Broad Gauge, 1892
Swindon Works, British Railways (Western Region) 1954, 1956, 1957
Swindon Works Open Day 1974, souvenir brochure
Swindon Works, published to commemorate the 125th anniversary of Swindon
  Locomotive Works and the centenary of Swindon Carriage and Wagon Works
Milestones for the Wonderful Western, Wiltshire Papers 1985
150 Great Western Railway Years, Kingfisher Railway Publications 1985
Swindon Works and its place in British Railway History, British Railway Engineering
  Ltd

Websites
http://andrewbriddonlocos.co.uk/abl2/
http://www.andrewgrantham.co.uk
http://www.bbc.co.uk/wiltshire/content/articles/2008/05/21/requiem_for_a_
  railway_swindon_films_80s_feature.shtml
http://www.british-history.ac.uk/vch/wilts/vol4/pp183-219#anchorn280
http://www.britishlistedbuildings.co.uk/en-318809-british-rail-engineering-limited-
  swindon#.VcDEf_mc7z1
http://www.john-ward.org.uk/personal/john/railways/index.html
http://locoperformance.tripod.com/edition20/swindonworks.htm
http://www.pastscape.org.uk/hob.aspx?hob_id=222111